WITHDRAWN

THE ITALIAN ELEMENT
IN MILTON'S VERSE

F. T. PRINCE

OXFORD
AT THE CLARENDON PRESS

Oxford University Press, Amen House, London E.C.4

GLASGOW NEW YORK TORONTO MELBOURNE WELLINGTON
BOMBAY CALCUTTA MADRAS KARACHI LAHORE DACCA
CAPE TOWN SALISBURY NAIROBI IBADAN ACCRA
KUALA LUMPUR HONG KONG

FIRST PUBLISHED 1954
REPRINTED LITHOGRAPHICALLY IN GREAT BRITAIN
AT THE UNIVERSITY PRESS, OXFORD
FROM CORRECTED SHEETS OF THE FIRST EDITION
1962

PREFATORY NOTE

Some passages in this book have appeared in articles in the Review of English Studies *and in* English Miscellany. *My thanks are due to the Editors of these journals.*

I wish to record my particular gratitude to Professor B. A. Wright; without his interest and approval I might never have begun, or concluded, this study.

F. T. P.

University of Southampton
February 1953

NOTE TO THE SECOND IMPRESSION

A second impression has enabled me to make a number of small corrections. These could not be extended to the last two sections of Chapter 8, though I now think that Milton's blank verse line is based upon a notional pattern of ten syllables alternately stressed and unstressed, in rising rhythm.

CONTENTS

CONTENTS

INTRODUCTION

THIS study was suggested by Dr. Johnson's observation that one of the sources of Milton's peculiar diction was 'his familiarity with the Tuscan poets: the disposition of his words is, I think, frequently Italian; perhaps sometimes combined with other tongues'. It proved to be impossible to confine the analysis, as it proceeded, to Milton's diction, for both prosody and diction turned out to be related to certain Italian experiments of the sixteenth century. My endeavour has been to show that this Italian influence on Milton's verse is deeper than it had been thought to be, especially as it affects the epic poetry.

Yet Milton's debt remains of a limited nature; and it should be clear that, however fully it is brought out, it does little to change our idea of Milton's relationship either to his Greek and Roman models or to his English predecessors. Virgil and Homer have always been acknowledged to be Milton's chief mentors. So far from displacing them from this position, an investigation of the Italian element in his verse confirms them in it. Milton turned to those Italian poets of the Renaissance who shared his purpose of reproducing the beauties of ancient poetry in vernacular speech. What he found in them, and what he could not have found in any other modern language, was a variety of verbal and metrical devices which they had worked out with the help of earlier Italian poetry, but with their eyes fixed on the new literary ideals. These experiments were useful to Milton because they were in a modern language, nearer to his own in syntax and idiom than Greek or Latin, and in a tradition of prosody which had already been proved capable of giving something to English verse. But in taking over what he found useful from this Italian school of writing, he never lost sight of his prime object, the emulation of Greek and Latin poetry.

The epic blank verse and the mature sonnets are most obviously and deeply marked by Italian experiments. In those more lyrical parts of his poetry which have been affected by the *canzone* and its derivatives, Milton prefers to use a greater freedom, and he sometimes deliberately seeks a final effect which differs widely from anything in Italian, as in the choruses of *Samson Agonistes*. In order to make clear these varying degrees of relationship it has been necessary to concentrate on the central theme, and to illustrate it with close analysis and detailed quotation. The Italian literary background has also been indicated, sometimes when it is not directly relevant to Milton's ultimate achievement, because only in this way can one make clear the distinct Italian school of writing which interested Milton most—the tradition of the Heroic Poem and epic 'magnificence' of style. And only in this way, too, is it possible to place the whole matter in its true perspective and so indicate how Milton took precisely what he needed, separating it with a wonderful instinct and insight from a mass of other suggestions and effects.

In nothing does his literary genius appear more plainly than in this discrimination. It is this which would explain, if explanation were needed, why he owes what he does to writers who are all in some way (and some in many ways) inferior to himself. But in fact this debt from the greater to the lesser needs no explanation. All great poets have learnt from poets less than themselves; if they had not had the capacity to do so, they would not have been, or become, great. If a

Dante, a Shakespeare, or a Milton is to learn only from his peers, how is he to learn at all? We know that in reality even the greatest works of such poets stand in a discernible relationship to inferior poetry of their own or earlier periods, even when the relationship discerned seems almost irrelevant, in view of the transformation that has taken place.

This transforming power is evident in all Milton's verse, whether it is applied to suggestions from Greek and Latin poets, from the Italians, or from his English predecessors. But it may be well to say something of the English background to his work, since the methods and limitations of this study may seem to set a false emphasis on its own subject.

Milton's achievement would have been possible at no earlier stage of the English tradition. The vigour and luxuriance of Elizabethan poetry prepared his way, gave the language a wealth of poetic resources which enabled it to support a rigorous artistic discipline such as that he imposed. Had his instrument not been exercised in the varied native strength and delicacy of Shakespeare and Spenser, Milton could never have hoped to become the poet of *Paradise Lost*. And if we like to plumb more deeply the wells of English poetry we may say that Shakespeare's verse might never have attained its own perfection of dramatic speech if new possibilities had not been opened up by Spenser; and that Spenser's greatness was founded upon the rediscovery of Chaucer, the discovery that Chaucer's diction and verse might be of practical value to sixteenth-century English.[1]

---

[1] It is significant that the great technical advances made by Chaucer and Spenser were in each case associated with a strong stimulus from French and Italian (as well as Latin) poetry. It seems that the mixed substance of the English language makes it a peculiarly flexible instrument; and that suggestions from foreign languages, and particularly the Romance languages, can thus very easily take effect.

Unfortunately, an investigation of Milton's place in this great unfolding of the English genius for poetry cannot be made on the same scale or by the same methods as an investigation of his 'debts' to Greek or Latin or Italian or Hebrew literature. One can attempt to trace the latter, as this study attempts to trace one of them, by means of a minute scrutiny of the texts. Milton's relation to earlier English poetry does not respond in the same way to such treatment. But the fact that his relation to Italian, say, does so respond, does not imply that it is more important than his relation to earlier poetry in his own language: it implies the opposite. Greek, Latin, Italian, Hebrew provided Milton with various means of constructing and moulding his epic works, whether these means were a method of narrative, a conception of poetic rhetoric, a sense of the music and movement of the verse, or details of metaphor, phrase, and cadence. But, just as his learning in those languages and cultures could not have given him, of itself, the living apprehension of his religious theme which sustains the whole, so it could never have given him the essential gift of a poet, which is a personal feeling for his own language.

Criticism has for so long assumed that great poetry can only be written in a poet's native language, that we have perhaps lost sight of what this assumption implies, and what it must imply even in the case of a poet who, like Milton, takes as his chief models poems written in alien idioms. It implies above all that the springs of intense creative energy in poetry lie so deep in the poet's being that they can only be tapped when he composes in the language which is his natural means of expression, which is the medium in which he lives. A poet's present and past environment, the present and past situation of his country, press continually on his act of creation, which is an act of intense and sustained consciousness, but which coexists with deep unconscious life. The poet lives in and through his own language, whether in intimate or formal personal relationships, or in reading, writing, speaking, think, ing, or dreaming. Unless he has, and keeps and de, velops, a gift for poetic expression in this language, he may make finished poems on a small scale in Greek or Latin (or in his own tongue), but he will never be capable of the intense and sustained effort which great poetry requires. Milton's diction and verse made an obvious effort to emulate certain features of Greek, Latin, and Italian poetry; but he succeeded in this emulation only because he had an incomparable in, stinct for English. We know that he had a remarkable insight into the qualities of those other three languages: but this was only one manifestation of a special genius for language, which reached its full power only in his own.

All this must be borne in mind when we attempt to estimate the relative importance to Milton of the Eng, lish poetic tradition and of such connexions as may be traced with Italian. And in view of the living, in, calculable nature of a poet's sense of his own tongue, the English background must be reckoned to include not only the whole body of literature in English, but also all other forms of expression in the English lan, guage that were available to Milton. Milton's capacities included not only intricate and formal writing but a gift for vivid and abundant colloquial speech, of which the prose of his middle years provides many examples. To confine ourselves, however, to poetry alone, and to the evidence of printed poetry: Milton was certainly in, fluenced by Elizabethan and later drama; we can find traces of minor dramatists, Fletcher or Middleton, as well as of Marlowe and Jonson. The influence of

Shakespeare alone is inestimable. Such evidence as we find seems, however, but slight and accidental when we conjecture the total poetic stimulus that Elizabethan drama would yield a young English poet of genius, born a few years before Shakespeare died. When we consider Milton's relation to Spenser we are on firmer ground, since Spenser was a poet of the same kind as Milton, a literary craftsman, who moreover anticipated many of Milton's interests and ambitions. Yet even here what cannot be traced and demonstrated must vastly outweigh what can be measured and seen on the surface.

Dryden reported Milton as saying that Spenser was his 'original'. Whatever Milton meant by this acknowledgement of his poetic ancestry, he cannot have meant that he derived from Spenser things of precisely the same order as those he derived from, let us say, Tasso. There is a demonstrable relationship between Milton's epic blank verse and the blank verse of Tasso. The formula for each was new in their respective languages; the formula for each is the same, with such differences as may be explained by the differing demands of English and Italian. There is no relationship of this kind between Milton and Spenser—or at least between Milton's blank verse and any verse of Spenser. If there had been, it would surely have been made clear long ago by one of the many scholars who have worked on the relationship between the two poets.

What Milton meant must therefore have been something different, and there is little doubt that it was something deeper and more farreaching. Milton may have meant that Spenser was the only English poet who had anticipated him in the ideal of a learned poetry dedicated to high spiritual and national ends; he may have meant that the lingering, intricate music of *The Faerie Queene* anticipated the music of his own verse, for the enormous exploitation of the aural qualities of the language by Spenser is the only earlier example in English of such writing as his own; he may well have meant that it was the experience of reading Spenser which first made him aware, as a child, of his own poetic vocation; he may even have meant that, just as Spenser had set himself to rival and 'overgo' the poetry of the Renaissance abroad, and had adopted some French and Italian methods of emulating Greek and Latin, he himself had continued and accomplished this task. Milton may have meant all this and more, for all this is no more than we can see for ourselves or conjecture with probability. The deep affinities between Spenser and Milton have always been recognized; even the publisher of the *Poems* of 1645 could claim that Milton was

'as true a Birth, as the Muses have brought forth since our famous *Spencer* wrote; whose Poems in these English ones are as rarely imitated, as sweetly excell'd.'

The moral kinship between the two poets must be left aside as not the concern of this study, though it is certainly as profound and was probably as important to Milton as anything more technical. But it is the technical relationship with which we are concerned, and certainly we can see that it is important enough to justify Milton's description of Spenser as his poetic 'father'.[1] Two of the possible implications of this statement seem particularly relevant, and they are closely related to each other: his probable reading of Spenser in childhood and his peculiar sensibility to the aural properties of English speech. In a highly cultivated Puritan household such as his father's, Milton would probably

[1] The seventeenth-century meanings of the word 'original' included that of 'ancestor' or 'father'.

not have had to wait until his school-days to become acquainted with at least some parts of *The Faerie Queene*; but he would certainly have come to know Spenser's verse, and to look at it closely, in his school-days, for Alexander Gill, High Master of St. Paul's in Milton's time, evidently made much use of Spenser in his teaching of English grammar and rhetoric.[1] Milton would have been taught to analyse Spenser's poetic diction, and to appreciate with what minute care Spenser had sought to devise in English methods of writing which would correspond to Virgil's style in Latin. One of the chief technical problems of epic verse, in the view of Renaissance critics, was to suit the sound of the poetry to the sense, 'to express by the quality of the verse the subject with which it was concerned'.[2] Virgil was acknowledged and recommended as the master of such writing. And Milton would have been taught to regard Spenser as the chief example in English, as he was, of a poet who had attempted to mould the language in this way.

Such an early appreciation of Spenser's diction would help to explain why it is that Milton's mature sense of language retains an affinity with Spenser's: an affinity which emerges clearly if we compare the idiom of these two poets—their vocabulary, their syntax, their use of metaphor, and so on—with that of Shakespeare. The strong individuality of Milton's mature style does not weaken the link with Spenser. The germinative power of Spenser's poetry has been shown repeatedly by the examples of later poets who have been able to

---

[1] 'Gill published a revised edition of his *Logonomia Anglica* in 1621, the year after Milton entered St. Paul's', writes Miss Helen Darbishire in her Introduction to *The Manuscript of Milton's Paradise Lost, Book I* (Oxford, 1931), p. xxxiii. In this grammar of the English language Gill frequently uses quotations from Spenser to exemplify figures of speech, including onomatopoeia.   [2] See p. 21.

find their own music with its help, or under its influence. Chatterton, Keats, Shelley, and Tennyson,
responding in diverse ways to Spenser, enriched and
developed their individual styles. Milton's earlier and
closer affinity to Spenser goes much farther; but it is
even more obviously an example of a lesson learnt by
a pupil who has thus been able to develop his own
individuality in verse. Milton's type of verbal music has
deep roots in *The Faerie Queene*: but his verse reaches
maturity by seeking a consistent and emphatic grandeur which is not one of the chief characteristics of
Spenser's style, though there were many examples of it
throughout his work.

All such connexions as that between Spenser and
Milton are in their nature almost impossible to define,
for they take effect at levels of consciousness which we
cannot penetrate. Coleridge tells us that some twenty
lines from Crashaw's *Hymn to St. Teresa*

were ever present to my mind whilst writing the second part of
Christabel; if, indeed, by some subtle process of the mind they
did not suggest the first thought of the whole poem.

Would we have been able to establish such a connexion without Coleridge's own statement? We may
make something of it—even a great deal—when we
have it; but it is something we could never have
deduced from *Christabel* as it stands. Such subtle influences may indeed come to a poet from other languages than his own; but it is in his own language
that they will play most constantly and with most delicate and various effect. The shadowy region in which
these things happen must be included in any complete
view of Milton's English background; it is altogether
beyond the reach of this study, which deals with something specific and limited and of a different order.

I

THE ITALIAN BACKGROUND

I

To define the total extent of Milton's debt to Italy is not within the scope of this study; such a task would require an almost inestimable volume of knowledge, and would very soon transgress the limits of a purely literary investigation. Italy was the source of Renaissance art and learning; throughout the greater part of the fifteenth and sixteenth centuries her intellectual influence was dominant in Europe, and even after the chill and the shadow which fell upon her culture in the latter part of the sixteenth century, she continued not only to produce magnificent works of art but also to advance humanist learning by exact studies and criticism. The Counter-Reformation itself was the heir of Renaissance culture, and in its turn exerted its influence, though an influence of less vitality and of diminished scope, over as much of Europe as remained within the sphere of the Catholic Church.

It would therefore be an undertaking of the greatest difficulty to distinguish the Italian contribution to the thought of a poet like Milton, who carries so great a weight of humanist and religious learning, and who remains, throughout all the vicissitudes of his century, a man of the later Renaissance. It would be less difficult, although by no means easy, to investigate as a whole the purely literary part of his debt: to consider, that is to say, not only direct relationships between his poetry and Italian poetry, but also his total debt to Italian literary theory of the sixteenth century.

Even this more limited purpose would, however, go farther than the present study, which sets out to describe only the part played by Italian writing in the formation of Milton's mature epic manner. The relationship between what we call 'Miltonic diction' and Italian poetry has never been fully explored. English scholars have been content to assume that Milton's peculiar idiom, devised in order to rival and reproduce the grand manner of Greek and Roman epic verse, was a personal invention. No doubt the fact that many of his procedures, and some indispensable technical principles, can be traced to Italian sources is of secondary importance. Milton's epic verse is ambitious of a direct challenge to Homer and Virgil; it invites, and can bear, the comparison. But we shall overestimate Milton's technical originality if we do not appreciate the degree to which his verse and diction rely upon the experiments and achievements of Italian poets of the Renaissance.

It would appear, and this study should make it appear, that Milton's style stands in particular in a very precise relationship to the verse of two poets, Giovanni Della Casa and Torquato Tasso. These two writers belong to different generations, and there are striking superficial differences between them. Della Casa was born in 1503 and died in 1556; Tasso was born in 1544 and died in 1595. The earlier poet left one of the smallest and most condensed collections of verse of any notable writer of the century, the later was one of the most productive poets of his own or any age. But Tasso owed some of the most used devices of his epic style to Della Casa's experiments within the narrow limits of the sonnet. Della Casa's contribution to the formation of the Italian idea of the 'magnificent' style was of fundamental importance; and this was the style that, described and applied by Tasso, was recreated in his own language by Milton.

If Milton is thus indebted to Tasso, Tasso is almost equally indebted to Della Casa in the particular matter of diction and prosody. But the interrelationships of the three poets do not end there, for Milton is indebted to Della Casa not only indirectly, through his greater successor, but directly: Milton's sonnets show that he took as his prime models the sonnets of Della Casa and not the less polished imitations of them produced by Tasso in his *Heroic Sonnets*.

Tasso's construction of an epic style with the help of some hints from Della Casa is reflected in critical essays by himself and others; the theory of diction he formed is fully discussed in one of his *Discorsi del Poema Eroico*, which is no doubt the form in which it became available to Milton. As an aid to the recreation of this epic style in English Tasso's criticism must have been invaluable, for it enables the reader to take his style to pieces and to isolate and estimate the effect of certain principles as they are applied in the text of the *Gerusalemme Liberata* or the *Mondo Creato*. The critical documents are essential to an understanding of Milton's view of Tasso.

II

It is also necessary, in order to understand the discoveries and experiments of Della Casa and Tasso, to have a general notion of the literary movement to which they belonged. To see them as mere individual innovators in the enormous and diverse literary production of the *Cinquecento* is not enough: they belong in fact to that renewal of Italian verse and prose which began in the early part of the century under the influence of Bembo. The essence of the work of Della Casa and of Tasso is that, in ways of their own but in company with all the major writers of the century, they sought to raise Italian literature to the level of accom﹣plishment of Latin and Greek: and it was Bembo who, by theory and example in the early years of the century, made it possible to undertake this task with some hope of success.

Bembo's *Prose della Volgar Lingua*, published in 1525, but begun more than twenty years before, determined the course of Italian fine writing for more than two hundred years. These dialogues established the Tuscan writers of the fourteenth century as the source of correct literary usage, and at the same time asserted the possi﹣bility of emulating in this literary language the glories of classical Greek and Latin literature. Bembo opened the way to a vast field of neo﹣classical experiment in Italian. A large part of the *Prose* is of course of relevance only to the study of Italian literature. But there are to be found in these critical discussions certain assumptions and conclusions concerning the new aesthetic ideals which throw light, not only on the poetry of the *Cinquecento*, but also on the poetry which Milton founded upon it. Thus Bembo's critical theories appear to be responsible for the curious para﹣dox that, while the poets and prose﹣writers who fol﹣lowed him accepted Tuscan of the fourteenth century as correct and desirable idiom, they at the same time attempted to mould it into quite alien forms—to emu﹣late with the substance of Italian words the complex diction of Virgil, Horace, or Cicero. Here, surely, is the origin of the 'perverse and pedantic principle' which

Dr. Johnson found in Milton's style: 'he was desirous of using English words in a foreign idiom'.

Moreover, we can see in Bembo's critical preferences and arguments the results of the new aesthetic ideals when applied to vernacular literature. These new ideals were of course founded entirely on the literature and criticism of Greece and Rome; applied to the great Italians of the fourteenth century, they give a new valuation. The immense superiority of Dante is discounted, and Petrarch becomes the idol of a new school of fine writing and artificial sentiment. Both the weakness and the strength of the new aesthetic ideals are indicated when we point out that they were above all literary. They made possible the creation of great literary epics, the *Gerusalemme Liberata* or *Paradise Lost*, by poets of exceptional powers; but they encouraged minor talents to treat literature as a self-justified activity, with the rules and assumptions of an elaborate game, and this could not but lead to an impoverishment of poetry in particular.

III

An intensely literary school or tradition of poetry will foster certain virtues: clarity, high finish and polish, intellectual deliberation and consistency, a fastidious taste. But it will be attended by certain dangers, always ready to entrap 'the practitioner of poetry': frigidity, a stiffness of approach to everyday experience and events, an inclination to substitute artistic formulae for emotion and vision. These characteristics marked the poetry of Bembo and his most faithful followers, and descended to the whole neo-classical tradition in Italy and Europe; they are present even in the greatest poets of that tradition, such as Milton.

The situation which preceded Bembo's mature writing, and the qualities of that writing itself, illustrate the distinction which he made between literary poetry, or the poetry of art, and Italian poetry as he found it. Italy at the end of the fifteenth century had no lack of poets; but their production was entirely for daily consumption, poetry of the court or of the market-place, poetry for recitation, poetry for singing, poetry as an element in riddling games or games of forfeits. Madrigals, *motti*, *strambotti*, and *capitoli*, *canti carnascialeschi*, and sonnets burlesque or serious—all this was social poetry, produced for immediate uses and aiming at immediate effects. The Petrarchan tradition had become debased, even in the work of the best of these poets, such as Serafino dell' Aquila. The chief narrative poem of the period, Boiardo's *Orlando Innamorato*, sprang equally from popular poetry, the chivalric epic, and had as little artistic purpose as the popular or courtly lyrics.

The absence of any high poetry at this time was undoubtedly due in part to the passion for Classical studies which had seized the most adventurous and disciplined minds. To write Latin verses of Augustan polish seemed the highest exercise open to a poetic gift; if the Latinists wrote poetry in Italian, as they often did, it was with no hope and no ambition of producing anything of lasting value. It was Bembo's achievement to put an end to this divorce between Classical learning and the vernacular.

No doubt the revival of high poetry in Italian was a natural development, which would have taken place sooner or later, without the concurrence of a critical theory such as Bembo provided. During the years in which Bembo meditated and polished the *Prose*, and in which his personal influence was felt in the literary circles of northern Italy, Ariosto conceived and composed the *Orlando Furioso*. His youth had been steeped in Classical poetry, and his great romantic epic effected a union between the popular tradition and the new learning which would in itself have sufficed to change the direction of Italian poetry. It is impossible to suppose that Ariosto would not have written his poem but for the opinion and approval of Bembo, so much smaller a poet than himself. But even he was grateful for Bembo's support and advice, and a host of lesser talents found in Bembo the literary programme they needed.

The *Prose* did not, therefore, affect the use of the vernacular for popular writing; for such purposes Italian was already used to extravagance, and continued to be so used throughout the sixteenth century. But Bembo's criticism initiated the poetry of the new learning, the poetry of art, in Italian; he restored the Petrarchan tradition in all its disciplined artifice, and gave Italian verse the means of setting out on new and ambitious experiments.

When Bembo points out the absurdity of trying to create fine literature in a dead language instead of in one's own living speech, he is supported by reason, instinct, and common sense. To perfect one's style in Latin, while neglecting Italian is, he says,

to make ourselves like those men who in some remote and uninhabited countryside, strive to erect enormous palaces, and elaborate and adorn them at great expense with gold and marble, while in the towns they live in they dwell in wretched tenements.

But such arguments, however sensible and logical, were of less value than the practical methods Bembo was able to provide for those who felt and thought as he did. These Renaissance critics and writers could scarcely conceive of literary composition except as imitation. If they were to write in Italian, they must be given authors to imitate. In order to know what authors to imitate, they must be given methods of discerning good from bad writing in Italian. The most important parts of the *Prose* are those in which Bembo shows that standards of judgement, and therefore methods of good writing, are in fact available in writing Italian, just as they are in writing Greek or Latin. He not only asserts this as an opinion, but he demonstrates it, and shows that he has arrived at it by way of exact knowledge: the First Book shows that he is familiar with Provençal poetry and is aware of its contribution to the poets of the *dolce stil nuovo*; the Second Book reveals his perception of the special linguistic qualities of Dante, Petrarch, and Boccaccio; the Third and Fourth Books exemplify the refinements proper to Tuscan writers and provide a summary grammar of the distinctive points of Tuscan usage.

In the course of this discussion of minute stylistic problems Bembo reveals his fundamental critical assumptions, and, prominent among them, the distinction between words and style which may assist our understanding of Milton.

In the Second Book the humanist Ercole Strozzi asks Carlo Bembo (who expresses the opinions of his brother the author) to explain to him

in what manner and by what rule judgement may be made, and by what mark good writings in the common tongue may be known from those not good; and of two works, which is better and which less good; and finally of that same form of composition among present-day Tuscans, of which we spoke yesterday, and which you say is not so good as that in which

Boccaccio and Petrarch wrote: why should one believe and decide this to be so?[1]

Carlo Bembo replies that 'the elements to be considered by one wishing to make this judgement' are 'in great measure the same as those to be considered in Latin compositions'. The 'material or subject' is one chief consideration, the 'form or appearance' is another. But, since they are not now discussing the 'material or subject', he continues,

speaking of this second part, I say, that every manner of writing is made up also of two elements: one of which is the choice, the other the arrangement, of the words.

The choice of words is not difficult. 'If one is expressing great matters,' they must be

grave, lofty, sonorous, emphatic and brilliant; if low and common things, they must be light, smooth, easy, quiet-sounding and in ordinary use; if the subject is of a middling nature between these two, the words too should be middling and temperate.

The arrangement of the words, however, is determined by more numerous and more complex considerations:

to dispose them well, it is not only necessary very often to compare one word with many other words; but rather to put together many forms of words with many other forms of words, and to compare them generally demands skill and practice.

Not only the order of the words is to be considered, but also their case, gender, and number, and whether they should be modified by means of elision or other devices. The two chief qualities of all writing, *gravità* and *piacevolezza*, must determine such decisions as these; and Bembo goes on to consider such factors as harmony,

---

[1] *Le Prose di Messer Pietro Bembo Cardinale, nelle quali si ragiona della Volgar Lingua . . .*, Divise in tre Libri (Verona, 1743), pp. 60–61.

'number', and variation, and to apply them to distinguish the 'grave' or 'pleasurable' properties of vowels
and consonants and rhyme-schemes.

The distinction between words and the arrangement
of words, between vocabulary and idiom, thus stands
at the head of Bembo's critical analysis, and makes
possible the chief literary effort of the century, the
cultivation of that *latinità in volgare* to which we find
a parallel in Milton. Without the example of Bembo's
followers Milton would never have succeeded as he did
in forming his epic diction, in which he uses all the
varied texture and substance of English words, but
exerts all his strength to work them into an un-
English structure.

One can understand why it has been said that the
triumph of Bembo's principles, far from representing
la rivincita della volgare, the 'come-back' of the common
tongue, really sealed the predominance of Greek and
Latin. Those writers who adhered closely to the programme did not in fact liberate Italian from the
apparently crushing superiority of the Classical languages, but rather attempted to impose on the modern
language as many of the procedures of the ancient as
it could be made to bear. Not only the artistic ideals of
the Classics (as they were then understood) were to
prevail; but the very details of their execution were to
be assimilated and imitated as closely as the idio-
syncrasies of a modern language would allow.

IV

Both in his analysis of the linguistic qualities of good
writing and in his more general critical judgements
Bembo is guided by the conception of literary decorum;
and it was under the supremacy of this ideal that most

of the forms of Italian poetry in the sixteenth century
flourished and were exhausted. It was by means of this
ideal that Bembo justified his exaltation of Petrarch
over Dante; and it is a conception eminently suited to
his sensibility and that of his school—a sensibility
exercised mainly in refinements of language or form,
and ready to put forward such refinements as the surest
basis of critical judgement. Thus Bembo declares that
those who prefer Dante to Petrarch are

swayed, as I think, by the greatness and variety of his subject,
more than by anything else; for the subject is indeed what makes
the poem (or at least may make it) high or low or average in
style; but good in itself, or not good, it never makes it.

The 'subject' is rendered of no more importance, or
even of less importance, than the execution, in which
the chief consideration has become the manner of preserving decorum. The notion of decorum in itself is
perhaps flexible enough to do no great harm; but in
alliance with an adulation of Greek and Roman literature, it proved fatal to the appreciation of most medieval
poetry. Dante's 'subject' was one which even the sixteenth-century humanists could not deny to be serious;
but they could not wholly approve of it because they
could find no precedent for it in the literature on which
they had formed their taste. They could no longer
appreciate his mastery instinctively, nor could they
justify it theoretically. Their conception of seriousness,
or *gravità*, in the long poem was now restricted to Greek
or Latin epic or tragedy.

The assimilation of Greek and Latin literature thus
led to a revaluation of existing Italian poetry; and in
the light of this revaluation Renaissance poets set their
course. The categorical distinctions of neo-classical
decorum were applied systematically to the Tuscan

tradition. Bembo declares that the value of all fine writing is determined by two factors, *gravità*, seriousness, and *piacevolezza*, pleasure. And it follows that in the Second Book of the *Prose* Dante's compositions are held to be 'grave, but without pleasure', as those of Cino da Pistoia are 'pleasant, without gravity'; and that in some of the work of these writers 'neither gravity nor pleasure is to be found'. Only one poet of the *Trecento* satisfies fully the logic of the new critical conceptions: for 'Petrarch fulfils marvellously' the demands of both gravity and pleasure, 'so that one cannot decide in which of the two he was the greater master'.

Thus Bembo was able, not only to imitate and develop Petrarch's manner—to which he was drawn by a kindred temperament and talent—but to justify by his critical theories the adoption of Petrarch as the chief Italian model for Renaissance poets. Artifice begins to predominate over vigour of conception and expression, and this process of decline is hastened by important changes in the mood and sensibility of the period. The misfortunes of Italy in the sixteenth century, the bewilderments of the Reformation and the Counter-Reformation, seem to be reflected in a loss of confidence and energy in the poetry of the period. Intense critical analysis plays its part in the general dissatisfaction. So Tasso produces his masterpiece under an obsessive shadow of critical and moral disapprobation; his own mental balance is disturbed, and the greater part of his creative force is wasted in misspent efforts, in a vain fight with critical abstractions. The disintegrating sensibility of the century is certainly traceable even in the *Gerusalemme Liberata*, where *piacevolezza* is tending towards prettiness, sentimentality, and sensuality, while *gravità*, undergoing a parallel

impoverishment, becomes sonority, exaggerated solem‑
nity, vague impressions of grandeur and horror.

Even Tasso's great epic is therefore scarcely worthy of
the high conception of the Heroic Poem which had
been formed by the criticism of the century and
attempted also by lesser poets. *Paradise Lost* was in fact
to be the European epic which realized the dreams of
Tasso and his predecessors, not only in its scale and its
religious intensity, but in the beauty of its poetic vision
and language. The Italian theories and experiments
had pointed the way; Milton brought to this literary
heritage the full heroic temper it required. In Italy
itself the 'magnificence' of the heroic style was not used
effectively until the later eighteenth century, when a
new national mood began to stir.

2

DELLA CASA
AND THE HEROIC SONNET

I

THE efforts of Bembo and his followers to enrich Italian verse with classic refinements were
made chiefly within the limits of the sonnet. The
reasons for this are obvious enough. Not only was the
sonnet the natural medium, at that time and for two or
three centuries to come, for the love-poetry which, no
less naturally, formed the bulk of Italian lyric verse; it
was also, by virtue of its limited scope and clear yet
complex structure, a form which could be carefully
polished, and one in which it was possible to concentrate upon small technical innovations and experiments.

The elaborate Latinate diction which was eventually
to emerge in Tasso's epic poetry therefore made its first
appearance in the sonnets of Bembo and Della Casa.
The position of the sonnet in relation to the development of epic diction is the same in the history of Italian
sixteenth-century poetry as it is in the work of Milton,
for in both cases the style which is to achieve such expansion is tested earlier on this small scale. Almost all
Milton's sonnets fall within the category of what Tasso
called 'Heroic Sonnets'—a form of which he himself
produced nearly five hundred examples. But Tasso was

alone in making a separate category for this type of sonnet and in exploiting it with such devastating thoroughness: the type of sonnet he calls heroic is best regarded as a by-product of the movement to latinize Italian verse which occupied the first half of the sixteenth century. Its antecedents may be found in Petrarch and Dante, but it is first given prominence by Bembo and raised to perfection by Della Casa.

Della Casa's innovations were distinctive and decisive. Bembo had already introduced into some of his sonnets a remarkable complexity and solemnity of diction. But an altogether new power of sustained rhythm appears in Della Casa, and makes possible an even bolder use of complexities of word-order.

In order to assess the precise degree of Della Casa's originality it will be well to give one or two examples of the complexity of diction already achieved by Bembo. The following sonnet by Bembo commends Vittoria Colonna for her poems in praise of her dead husband:

> Cingi le costei tempie dell' amato
>   Da te già in volto umano arboscel, poi
>   Ch'ella sorvola i più leggiadri tuoi
>   Poeti col suo verso alto e purgato:
> E se 'n donna valor, bel petto armato
>   D'onestà, real sangue onorar vuoi,
>   Onora lei, cui par, Febo, non puoi
>   Veder quaggiù, tanto dal ciel l'è dato.
> Felice lui, ch'è sol conforme obbietto
>   All' ampio stile, e dal beato regno
>   Vede, Amor santo quanto pote e vale:
> E lei ben nata, che sì chiaro segno
>   Stampa del marital suo casto affetto,
>   E con gran passi a vera gloria sale.[1]

---

[1] The sonnet is addressed to Apollo. 'Bind this lady's temples with the shrub beloved by thee once in human form [literally, 'with the

The poem can hardly be called anything but frigid, and the impression of semi-official compliment is only increased by the skilful contortion of phrase, particularly obvious in the quatrains. The sentences are manipulated carefully so as not to coincide with the line-endings; but they do not transgress the limits of the quatrains and tercets, and this is on the whole characteristic of Bembo's methods.

A slightly more personal, and even more characteristic, sonnet is that addressed to Nicolò Phrisio, a friend who has entered a monastery:

> Phrisio, *che già da questa gente a quella*
> *Passando vago, e fama in ciascun lato*
> *Mercando, hai poco men cerco e girato,*
> *Quanto riscalda la diurna stella;*
> *Ed or per render l'alma pura e bella*
> *Al ciel, quando 'l tuo dì ti sia segnato,*
> *Nel tuo ancor verde e più felice stato*
> *Ti chiudi in sacra e solitaria cella:*
> *Eletto ben hai tu la miglior parte,*
> *Che non ti si torrà: fossi anch' io a tale*
> *Nè mi torcesse empia vaghezza i passi:*
> *Contra la qual poi ch'altro non mi vale*
> *Pregal Signor per me tu, che mi lassi*
> *Senza te frale e sconsolata parte.*[1]

beloved by thee once in human form shrub'], since she soars above the most delectable of thy poets with her pure and lofty verse:

'And if thou wishest to honour in a woman courage, a fair breast armed in chastity, and royal blood, honour her, whose equal, Phoebus, thou canst not see on earth, so much has Heaven granted her.

'Happy he, who alone is a fitting object for her full style, and from the Kingdom of the Blest sees how much holy Love can do, and is worth;

'And she, the noble lady who forges so clear a mark of her chaste spousal love, and climbs with firm steps to true glory.' *Rime* (Roma, 1548), p. 97.

[1] 'Phrisio, who erstwhile passing pleasantly from this country to

The combination of formality and intimacy in this sonnet is one of the constant qualities of this type of poetry, and one which Milton hits exactly in many of his sonnets. Bembo here uses several devices which were to prove of lasting service: the name of the person to whom the sonnet is addressed is placed ceremoniously at the beginning; the apostrophe is continued in relative clauses which extend throughout the two quatrains; the thought and the syntax knit the tercets together in the same way. The whole effect is one of reflection and deliberate utterance, yet a certain abruptness, and the way in which the flow of the sentences overrides the divisions of the stanza, give a formal equivalent of spontaneous speech. Milton achieves the same general effect, in part by the very same means.

The reluctant worldliness and the helpless aspiration towards religious peace, expressed in this poem, are too frequent in this school of poetry not to be in some degree a convention deriving from Petrarch. But these themes are modulated into an echo of Horace, in the sonnets of Bembo and Della Casa, which often make an implicit claim to belong to the great world, the world of statecraft and personal ambition. This claim lingers, with little to justify it, in Tasso's *Heroic Sonnets*. Milton, involved deeply in national affairs during the

that, and in all regions winning fame, hast travelled through and circled scarce less than all that the day-star warms;

'And now, to render thy soul pure and fair to Heaven, when thy day is assigned to thee, in thy yet green and more flourishing state shutt'st thyself in a solitary and saintly cell:

'Thou hast indeed chosen the better part, which shall not be taken from thee: would I were [arrived] at such, and that ill desires did not guide my steps awry!

'Against which, since nothing else avails me, pray thou the Lord for me, that he may leave me a frail and comfortless lot, without thee.' Op. cit., p. 55.

period of his sonnet-writing, is able to take full advantage of this tradition in the Renaissance sonnets.

The movement and diction of the sonnet to Phrisio show Bembo at his best. Farther than this, in the direction of epic dignity and 'magnificence', he could not successfully go. The mood of his verse remains more elegiac than heroic.

It is clear that Bembo's place in the tradition which Milton took up is of considerable importance. But the full emergence of a new style, to be developed into an epic style by Tasso, was achieved only by Della Casa. Tasso himself did all he could to emphasize Della Casa's historic importance, which was confirmed by seventeenth-century Italian criticism, and has been indicated even in modern times by Italian literary historians.[1] A description of the novelties of Della Casa's verse, as they appeared to Italians in the latter part of the sixteenth century, will contribute to our understanding of what Tasso and Milton could derive from this minor poet.

II

A dialogue of uncertain authorship has survived, presumably from the late sixteenth century, in which Tasso is given the task of expounding the secrets of Della Casa's style and the way to imitate it.[2] Tasso had

---

[1] The Venetian edition, *Opere di Monsignor Giovanni Della Casa* (Venice, 1728), 5 vols., reprints a mass of sixteenth- and seventeenth-century comment.

[2] *Il Tasso, Dialogo d'Incerto, sopra lo stile di Monsignore Della Casa, e il modo d'imitarlo*: see Della Casa, op. cit., *Aggiunta di Alcune Cose Appartenenti al Primo Tomo*, pp. 8–19. The second person of the dialogue is Annibale Pocaterra, a young gentleman of the Court of Ferrara, to whom, and to whose father, Tasso addressed several of his *Heroic Sonnets*.

written with admiration of Della Casa's verse in more
than one passage of his prose, and some of these eulogies
were known to the author of this dialogue which bears
his name.[1] The dialogue itself confirms that Tasso was
recognized to be the chief advocate and imitator of
Della Casa's style in his own time, for it is generally
accepted that when Italian writers of dialogues made
use of contemporary characters they attributed to them
only opinions they really held and might well have expressed in private conversation. It cannot, of course,
be claimed that Milton knew this particular piece of
criticism; but it contains nothing that he might not
have been able to hear at meetings of the Italian
academies he frequented in 1638 and 1639.

Il Tasso begins with a definition of imitation, in
which the poet is made to draw a distinction between
exact imitation of a particular author, which is, he
believes, inevitable in writing Latin, and a more
emancipated kind of imitation which consists in
'following in the track of some illustrious writer' and
which may 'bestow the greatest skill on one who
wishes to write well'.[2] Della Casa is then put forward,
therefore, not as one whose style should be emulated as
an end in itself, but as one who can be of the greatest
help in composing good poetry 'in so far as he is more
polished than all the rest'. We have here a suggestion
of what was in fact Tasso's relation to this poet; he
sought to form a synthetic style to be used for poetry
of a kind not attempted by Della Casa—the Heroic
Poem—but for this purpose he thought it possible to
adapt the principles of Della Casa's style. The analysis

[1] There are references to Tasso's lecture on Della Casa's Sonnet
LIX and to *La Cavalletta*. The *Discorsi* and the reference to Della
Casa in the *Dialogue on Jealousy* are not mentioned.

[2] Op. cit., *Aggiunta*, p. 11. All the translated extracts are from this
source.

of these principles is the chief business of this dialogue; it is entirely consonant with the opinions put forward in Tasso's own *Discorsi*, and with the poetry he wrote to this formula.[1]

In order to show how accomplished a writer Della Casa is, the poet postulates that a writer's skill can appear, 'either making appear marvellous that which in itself is not so; or clothing the subject so magni‑ ficently that it appears as a great and excellent thing'. 'None knew better than Monsignor Della Casa how to do this; since any trite and common sentiment what‑ soever comes to be so ennobled by him, that it seems to be one of the most wonderful things that have ever been said.' Sonnet XXXV is a good example of this, 'in which he only mentions several ladies who were famous for their beauty, and adds: *if Paris were their judge, they would yield their place to his Lady*. This sentiment, which contains nothing great in itself, is so raised up by his style, that it becomes one of the rarest gems that our poetry owns, if I am not mis‑ taken.'

Our modern notions of the nature of poetry are so entirely opposed to this conception of its workings that such remarks sound almost comical. Yet they con‑ tribute something to our knowledge, not only of Tasso and Della Casa, but also of Milton; for, if it is true that many of Della Casa's finest sonnets are reared upon the basis of a few far from recondite reflections, this is true also of some of Milton's English sonnets.[2] And the idea that by verbal clothing of elaborate tissue an epic poem may be ennobled and sustained is surely one of the basic assumptions, not only of the *Gerusalemme Liberata*, but of *Paradise Lost*.

A further general observation on Della Casa's verse

[1] See pp. 36–43.   [2] See p. 105.

is made before the closer analysis; that 'he exerted himself to express by the quality of the verse the quality of
the subject with which it was concerned': which is 'the
usage of the most renowned poets of every age, and
above all of Virgil, than whom none was a more dili-
gent observer of this laborious task'.[1] Della Casa was
an industrious imitator of Virgil in this respect. 'Read
his Sonnet *Curi le paci sue chi vede Marte*, and admire
how in the quatrains, in which he speaks of winds,
tempests, waves, seas, he is great and majestic; and
in the tercets, in which he speaks with contempt
of mundane things, low and familiar.' Examples
are cited of verses which are sweet in the Petrarchan manner, or languid or lofty, according to the
theme.

But now comes the more technical part of the discussion. For 'the principal cause of the greatness and
loftiness of his style' lies 'in the wonderful skill he
showed in breaking up the verses, and in separating
the words which are commonly placed together'.
These two devices are thus regarded as distinctive of
Della Casa's manner, and they are dealt with at some
length.

'As for the breaking up of the verses', the critic declares, 'it cannot be denied that this is the first cause of
the elevated style. Read Virgil, and you will see how
frequently he places at the beginning of the succeeding
verse the word which completes the thought of its
predecessor.' Della Casa used this device more than
any previous poet in Italian, though no doubt he derived suggestions for it from Bembo and Petrarch. For

---

[1] 'And for this reason', he adds, 'Comendator Caro's translation
especially pleases me, that in this respect he spares himself no trouble,
but takes thought to follow Virgil and to express in the sound of the
verse the subject underlying it.' For the relation of Caro's *Eneide* to
Tasso's and Milton's epic blank verse, see p. 51.

'the same thing is to be observed in Bembo's poems',
and 'if I am not mistaken, Della Casa learned from
him that artifice, in which, employing all his efforts,
he achieved a marvellous grandeur . . . so that in this
he outwent not only Bembo but any other of our poets'.
Some examples are cited, and Tasso is made to justify
the practice by a comparison from Dionysius of Halicarnassus, which reappears in the *Discorsi del Poema
Eroico*.[1] It is plain from the emphasis placed on the
critical and poetic authority for this device that it was
far from meeting with universal approval. 'I have heard
some blame Mons. Della Casa, for using these transitions too often', the writer admits:[2] but he argues,
let people only admit that they were common in Latin
and Greek lyric and elegiac poetry, and then they may
freely admire the magnificent use Della Casa makes of
them.

   The second distinctive feature of Della Casa's manner is advocated on similar grounds, and has also to be
defended against critical objections. The distortion of
the natural word-order (*lo scompigliare o disunir delle
voci*) is, 'if it be done with judgement, a most important
means to magnificence in style'. Della Casa in this
excelled all others, and

applying every effort to make the device his own, he so succeeds that in his lofty and solemn diction he make us feel an
indefinable quality of severity which pleases us, a stiffness which
is yet highly delightful; and the reason why this separation of the
words thus makes the style elegant and can endow it with such
force and animation, I believe to be that, if, as Quintilian says,

   [1] See p. 39.
   [2] Some critics condemned outright the 'breaking up of the verses'
in sonnets: 'Non si possono senza biasimo far cavalcar le Sentenze
da una Stanza all' altra, nè da un Quaternario, o da un Terzetto al-
l'altro, ma rinchiuderle ne' suoi confini' (Stefano Guazzo, quoted
in Della Casa, *Opere* (Venice, 1728), i. 184).

a style is solemn and severe and ornate in proportion to its departure from the common people and its remoteness from their ordinary manner of speech, that style will be much more so which takes for its first purpose the avoidance of usual expressions, and seeks out the most far-fetched forms.

Della Casa took the utmost care to avoid by these means trite formulas of speech and writing. 'You cannot read any of his sonnets or *canzoni* without perceiving the infinite accuracy with which he breaks up the phrases, and, having divided them gracefully into several parts, reassembles the words in the most appropriate and eloquent positions.' A few brief examples are given, but these are tokens rather than adequate illustrations, since the whole of this poet's language is distinguished by its intricacy of syntax, and only the quotation of entire poems can give an impression of his mastery of such devices.

The critic proceeds to justify this interference with the natural word-order by referring to the elaboration of Cicero's prose, but his interlocutor makes an objection which must occur to anyone who compares the relative capacities of Latin and a modern language in this particular. 'I grant you', the objector says, 'that in Latin, which admits of much hyperbaton, the writer is free to move away from his everyday self and seek this solemn and sustained manner: but how can that be done in the vulgar tongue, since that admits of but a slight degree of transposition of words, such as we find in the *Decameron* of Boccaccio or the prose of Monsignor Bembo?' But the answer is ready and, it must be admitted, not ineffective. It is true that there is a difficulty here, replies the critic, though it is less serious in poetry than in prose; but there is good reason to think that Italian can obtain an equivalent to the Latin style. For it has already been laid down that a style is more lofty as it departs farther from common speech: and, 'if in order to attain this end in our language it is sufficient to transpose the words but moderately (since transposition is not so frequent as it is in Latin), why will you not agree that the style of some Tuscan authors may be as elegant in this respect with a slight transposition of words, as the style of Latin authors is with a greater?'

Such an argument as this is highly relevant to Milton's effort to reproduce in English the effects of Latinate grandeur aimed at by Della Casa and later by Tasso. The relative lack of inflexions in English hampered Milton in reproducing some distortions of the natural word-order which were devised by Della Casa: he could not but use such devices less boldly. But as the Italians argued in comparing their language with Latin, so could he argue in comparing English with Latin and Italian. If English allowed less free-dom than either, for that very reason a slighter degree of distortion would avail to produce an equivalent effect of strangeness. The value of Della Casa's verse to Milton was that it showed him that a modern lan-guage could indeed rival the complex word-order of Latin, and gave him many suggestions as to the verbal patterns he could use for this purpose.

When it is considered in conjunction with Tasso's *Discorsi* and his heroic poetry, *Il Tasso* shows that Della Casa was the chief Italian model for the 'magnificent' style which Tasso evolved, and which in its turn con-tributed to the formation of Milton's epic manner. It is remarkable that such a position in the development of a great epic style should be held by so small a collection of verse as Della Casa's, some seventy sonnets in all; and their quality in fact warrants fuller appreciation than the technical analysis in *Il Tasso* provides.

III

Not only the extreme artifice of the style, but the 'subject' of much of Della Casa's verse, makes little appeal to modern taste. The larger part of his poetic production, like that of Bembo, consists of love sonnets which, despite their novelties of diction, fall well within the conventions of the Petrarchan tradition. It would be possible to study the latinization of the style in these love-poems as well as in the sonnets of compliment and reflection; but there is naturally a slightly greater infusion of heroic dignity into the latter, and it is more profitable to concentrate upon these for the further reason that Milton wrote no sonnets of Petrarchan sentiment (except for those in Italian).

Moreover, like many another Petrarchan love-poet, and perhaps like Petrarch himself, Della Casa writes more moving poetry when he withdraws a certain distance from the object of his emotions and makes his poem a moral reflection on his own state of mind and way of life. We have here a process implicit in Petrarch's type of love-poetry, and one which accounts for the emergence of the Heroic Sonnet from that tradition. Petrarchan poetry rests ultimately on a Christian idea, the analogy and the conflict between human love and the love of God. Petrarchan poets therefore use the sonnet partly as a vehicle for the expression of the psychology of love, partly for the expression of something more abstract, a system of religious values. Della Casa is most convincing when he moves into the region of moral reflection, and refers to love, as he refers to his worldly ambitions, merely as an intense and lamentable experience.

Most of these sonnets, of varying degrees of candour and intimacy, are addressed to friends, fellow poets, or patrons; some express grief at a friend's death; some are religious meditations, and a few record indignant thoughts on the troubles of Italy in the mid-century. Most refer to disappointed ambitions, the struggle for personal happiness or power. The most detached and austere were written in the poet's last years, when the failure of his ecclesiastical ambitions was no longer in doubt, and he had retired to Venice or Treviso. The seriousness of Della Casa's mood at this time is exemplified in the following sonnet addressed from Venice to a friend in Florence:

> Feroce spirto un tempo ebbi e guerrero,
>   E per ornar la scorza anch' io di fore,
>   Molto contesi; or langue il corpo, e 'l core
>   Paventa: ond' io riposo, e pace chero.
> Coprami omai vermiglia vesta, o nero
>   Manto, poco mi fia gioia, o dolore;
>   Ch'a sera è il mio dì corso, e ben l'errore
>   Scorgo or del vulgo, che mal scerne il vero.
> La spoglia il Mondo mira. Or non s'arresta
>   Spesso nel fango augel di bianche piume?
>   Gloria non di virtù figlia che vale?
> Per lei, Francesco, ebb' io guerra molesta;
>   Ed or placido, inerme, entro un bel fiume
>   Sacro ho il mio nido, e nulla altro mi cale.[1]

[1] Sonnet XLVIII. 'A fierce spirit one time I had, and warlike, and to adorn the outward husk I too contended greatly; now body languishes and heart trembles: whence I repose and peace implore.

'Henceforth let scarlet robe or black mantle cover me, little joy or sorrow will it bring me; for to evening my day has drawn, and clearly now I see the error of the common people, who but ill discern the truth.

'The dress the world regards. Now, may not oft-times a bird of white plumage be caught in mud? What avails glory [that is] not daughter of virtue?

'For her sake, Francesco, I made wretched war; and now, placid and disarmed, in [the bosom of] a fair river I have my sacred nest, and naught else recks me.'

In this sonnet we see all the complexity of word-order already found in Bembo,[1] but carried farther with the help of a slower, more weighty rhythm. This new rhythm derives in part from methods which Bembo also used, such as the 'breaking up of the verses' by placing 'at the beginning of the succeeding verse the word which completes the thought of its predecessor'.[2] But it is enhanced by two new devices, the placing of strong pauses within the lines, and the deliberate accumulation of elisions. Neither of these two devices is explicitly mentioned by the author of *Il Tasso*, who may not have been poet enough to detect their full importance. They are, however, among those features of the 'magnificent' style expressly described by Tasso himself in the *Discorsi*, and applied by him in the texture of his own epic verse. And they pass into the prosody of Milton's blank verse, giving it a stamp and structure until then unknown in English poetry.[3]

Tasso introduces examples of these new rhythms and elisions into his description of *asprezza*, 'roughness' or 'difficulty', which he considers an essential quality in epic verse.[4] In Della Casa's style this difficulty is the distinctive and decisive factor. There is no theme in his repertory which is entirely his own; he has no manner of contemplating his experience or communicating it to others which has not been used a hundred times by Petrarch, by Bembo, or by his nearer contemporaries, Varchi, Bernardo Capello, Berardino Rota, and the rest. Yet he contrives to infuse a new reality into all these commonplaces of judgement and sentiment. And one of his methods which can be detected and isolated is precisely this invention of a new weight and diffi-culty of utterance in verse. His artifices might be

---

[1] See the sonnet to Phrisio, p. 16.   [2] See p. 21.
[3] See p. 132.   [4] See p. 38.

expected to emphasize the conventionality of poetic speech and not its possible sincerity. In fact the *asprezza* they produce has the effect of conveying and confirming the poet's seriousness, as if we felt that difficult poetry must be more intimate and exact than facile.

Such a result could follow only from a special poetic instinct, the power to embody emotion and sensation in word and syllable. But we can relate this instinct to the poet's temperament, which must have had a certain active soundness of moral sensibility. Della Casa's poetry is perhaps to be regarded as a triumph of courtesy: his treatise of good manners, the *Galateo*, ex, pressed an ideal of good taste far beyond the reach of most of his contemporaries, and personal insight reigns also in the sonnets. Many of them are in origin compli, mentary verses, and one need only compare them with most of the complimentary verse of the period to find that there is here a discrimination of quite remarkable purity. Nothing is said that is not at once measured, appropriate and pleasing; everything is in a sense ex, pected, yet nothing is without an air of freshness and conviction.

As examples of this conveyance of deep feeling by finished poetic artifice, one might point to two sonnets on the death of Trifon Gabriele, and two on the death of a closer friend, Marcantonio Soranzo. One of the latter illustrates also Della Casa's manner of referring to worldly cares and desires:

> Il tuo candido fil tosto le amare
> Per me, Soranzo mio, Parche troncaro:
> E troncandolo, in lutto mi lassaro;
> Che noia, quant' io miro, e duol m'appare.
> Ben sai, ch'al viver mio, cui brevi e rare
> Prescrisse ore serene il ciel avaro,

Non ebbi altro, che te, lume, o riparo:
Or non è chi 'l sostenga, o chi 'l rischiare.
Bella fera e gentil mi punse il seno:
E poi fuggìo da me ratta lontano,
Vago lassando il cor del suo veneno;
E mentre ella per me s'attende invano,
Lasso, ti parti tu, non ancor pieno
I primi spazi pur del corso umano.[1]

This vision of his own life and of the lives of others, through the transparence of a religious sorrow, is the finest motive of Della Casa's sonnets; and it is interest-ing to consider the relation of this unique poetry, not only to his personal sensibility and social ideals, but to the conception of literary decorum. The very limited value and the very real dangers of this conception, both for criticism and for creation, are clear. Yet it certainly plays no small part in the exquisite balance of forces which underlies Della Casa's verse.

In Milton we have the only great English poet whose work is based on the same literary and social sense of decorum. To read Milton's sonnets with attention to their content is to see how, as in Della Casa, the com-monplace is touched to glory by a deep earnestness; and the notion of decorum similarly pervades the epics.

[1] Sonnet XII. 'Thy white thread, my Soranzo, swiftly the Fates, bitter to me, cut off [literally, "swiftly the bitter, for me, Soranzo mine, Fates cut off"]: and in so cutting it left me in grief; for weariness and pain appear, wherever I look.

'Thou well know'st that in this my life, to which the niggard sky prescribed few and scattered hours of peace, I had no other light or support than thee: now there is none to sustain it or to lighten it.

'A lovely and gentle wild thing pierced my breast: and then fled from me swiftly afar, leaving my heart in love with her poison:

'And while I tarry for her in vain, alas, thou leav'st me, not yet having completed even the first stretches of our human course.'

The 'magnificence', the heroic gravity, the *asprezza*, of Della Casa's verse anticipated the mood of the later sixteenth century and inspired the chief poet of the Counter-Reformation, Tasso. It would seem that this poet's moral sensibility extended to a perception of the changing mood of his time, though the perception came too late to bring him any practical reward—if, indeed, it could ever have done so. It has often enough been pointed out that Della Casa discovered from bitter experience that the time had passed when it was possible to combine the brilliance and luxury of humanist learning with the demands of high office in the Church. Yet Della Casa might well have been sensitive in poetry to the atmosphere of his time, without being able for all that to make any practical use of his perceptions. The examples of Donne, Dryden, Byron, Baudelaire, and many others prove that 'modernity' may go together with a failure to come to terms with the needs of contemporary life. Such a failure may indeed be a condition of such a sense of the issues of one's time. Certainly Della Casa's poetry did not unfold its full capacity for solemn beauty, the heroic mood of the Counter-Reformation, until he had accepted the defeat of his ambitions in the Church.

IV

The appreciation of such poetry as Della Casa's perhaps demands a special feeling for language and form: as it is learned poetry, so it asks for a somewhat learned response, an awareness of careful modifications of tone and substance. That Milton had the necessary sense of form would be obvious (if it were not otherwise obvious) from the eagerness with which he emulated in Della Casa precisely those innovations which many found too bold.[1] It is not so obvious that critics of his, or Della Casa's, sonnets have shared this sense of form, and one may suspect that Tasso, for all his enthusiastic advocacy of Della Casa, lacked an equal discrimination.

Certainly Tasso's *Sonetti Eroici,* nearly five hundred in all, fail to outshine the mere handful left by his master. There seems to be only one feature that they could have contributed to Milton's conception of the uses of the sonnet, only one feature not already plainly given by Bembo or Della Casa: that is, the idea itself of an Heroic Sonnet, as a poem treating contemporary themes with epic grandeur, and celebrating, above all, the exploits of great leaders with whom the poet might claim some personal or official acquaintance. Tasso's *Heroic Sonnets* have this semi-public, semi-official note, like those of Milton to Cromwell, Fairfax, or Vane. Della Casa makes no such addresses to the great: the glory which surrounds, for example, his Farnese patrons is seen at one remove in his poems, seen always from his personal situation. Tasso's personal situation is also the motive of many of these sonnets; but too often he celebrates remote figures, and then can only in-dulge in excessive and hollow panegyric.

Yet even in these superabundant praises, sonnets to Ranuccio Farnese, Prince of Parma, to Don John of Austria, to the Grand Duke of Tuscany, the Duke of Savoy, and to countless cardinals, some strange per-sonal hallucination seems to be at work. Tasso's feeling for greatness has an aura of religion or superstition. The appeals he makes in his melancholy-madness to Alfonso d'Este and other rulers suggest a pathetic con-viction of the efficacy of worldly power, even in such

[1] See p. 106.

obscure afflictions as his own. He writes imploringly to
Duke Alfonso:

> Lasso! chi queste al mio pensier figura
>   Ora torbide e meste, or liete e chiare
>   Larve, colle quai spesso (o che mi pare)
>   Inerme ho pugna perigliosa, e dura?
> Opra è questa d'incanto, o mia paura
>   È la mia maga, e 'ncontro a quel ch'appare,
>   Pur quasi canna, o giunco in riva al mare,
>   Rende l'alma tremante, e mal sicura?
> O magnanimo Alfonso, omai disperga
>   Raggio di tua pietà, l'ombre, e gli errori,
>   E sia per me sovra le nebbie un Sole.
> E là mi guidi, ove Amor teco alberga
>   Tra larve usate in amorosi cori,
>   Sicchè la vista e gli occhi egri console.[1]

One cannot read far in these sonnets without meeting
innumerable echoes of Della Casa. Tasso's retentive
memory resounded with rhymes, phrases, images, and
geographical and mythological allusions drawn from
what was, compared with his own, a very small body
of writing. The *Heroic Sonnets* are not only an applica‑
tion, an extension, of Della Casa's style, but, not un‑

---

[1] *Al Duca di Ferrara, quando era Agitato da Malinconia* (Tasso, *Opere*
(Pisa, 1823), iv. 77).

'Alas! who shapes in my thoughts these phantoms, now dis‑
turbed and sad, now joyful and clear, with which oft-times (or
so it seems to me) without weapons I join in dangerous and hard
battle?

'Is this worked by enchantment, or is it my fear that is a sorceress
to me, and in the face of things I see, makes my soul trembling and
insecure, even as a reed or a rush on the shore of the sea?

'O noble Alfonso, henceforth may a ray of thy mercy disperse
the shadows and the errors, and be to me as a sun above the
clouds.

'And may it guide me there where Love dwells with thee
among such spirits as are found in choirs of love, so that he may
console my sight and my ailing eyes.'

naturally, a vulgarization of it. Tasso makes use almost exclusively of the more imitable, more external, features of 'magnificence'. He can easily use the imagery, vocabulary, involved and often obscure wordorder, and harsh and heavy rhymes, of his models; but he cannot so easily attain, and seldom attempts, the rhythmic subtlety which is of such inestimable value. Tasso almost never adopts that modulation of movement which comes from an overflow of sentences from quatrain to quatrain, or quatrains to tercets, which Della Casa used so deliberately.[1]

It was natural that Tasso should have stopped short of this effect, and also of the kindred device of emphasizing strong pauses within the lines. Such rhythms would have been incompatible with his fluency, which is based upon an essentially mechanical use of the movement of the sonnet. One of the chief virtues of Della Casa's rhythmic innovations had been to counteract the dangerously mechanical tendency of the form, giving it a new lease of life at a time when its possibilities might have seemed to be exhausted. Milton would never have been able to make the sonnet one of the vehicles of his own type of poetry, if he had not in this respect followed Della Casa, and not his disciple Tasso.

[1] Nos. 198 and 446 are examples of this licence in the *Sonetti Eroici*: practically negligible in the total bulk of these poems.

3

TASSO AND THE EPIC

I

TASSO's high place in the tradition of Renaissance Christian Epic makes his work of obvious
relevance to Milton's achievement. But the striking dissimilarity between the *Gerusalemme Liberata* and
Paradise Lost may well have diverted attention from the
deeper relationship between the two poets. There is
both a contrast and a certain affinity between Tasso's
religious mood, dominated by the intellectual revolu-
tion of the Counter-Reformation, and Milton's much
bolder, narrower, and more personal, religious opinions.
Tasso, if not so learned as Milton, must be reckoned
a learned poet; they both attempt a synthesis between Renaissance philosophy and Christian tradition.
Moreover, a certain resemblance appears in the deeply
emotional quality which they give their intellectual
synthesis. This is obvious in the romantic melancholy
which pervades the *Gerusalemme Liberata*. It is less obvious in *Paradise Lost*, which has a greater severity of
manner and a higher degree of dogmatic consistency;
but Milton too reveals a quality and intensity of emotion which might be called romantic.

Yet the most definite and important relationship
between the two poets is undoubtedly that of their
technique: Milton owes an immense debt to Tasso's
instructions and experiments in epic diction. In order to

estimate this one must take into account, not only the *Gerusalemme Liberata*, but the *Discorsi* and the long blank-verse poem of Tasso's last years, the *Sette Giornate del Mondo Creato*. The evidence of all these combined shows that Milton's style profited from Tasso's practice as much as from his theories.[1]

In Tasso's work as a whole all the important neo-classical developments in the poetry of the earlier sixteenth century met and combined in new forms, most of which are relevant, in one way or another, to the study of Milton.[2] Thus in the formation of Tasso's 'magnificent' style Della Casa's verse played a decisive part, and the full historical importance of Della Casa's innovations lies rather in the use Tasso made of them than in their direct effect on other poets. Della Casa's experiments in the sonnet had no wide or lasting in-fluence on sonnet-writing in Italy, which continued on rather more Petrarchan lines. But Tasso adapted what he could of the Della Casan manner in the *ottava rima* of the *Gerusalemme Liberata*; and he gave it an even wider currency, under a new guise, when he devised with its help the blank verse of the *Mondo Creato*, which Milton re-created in English and which was carried to further achievements by Parini and Foscolo in Italy in the eighteenth century.

[1] Professor Mario Praz does full justice only to one aspect of this debt, when he writes: 'Certainly, among the Italian authors who influenced Milton, Tasso . . . deserved the place of honour, by virtue rather of his theories than of his effective example. The precepts which Tasso usually put on one side when inspiration visited him . . . were followed methodically by Milton.' *Rapporti tra la letteratura italiana e la letteratura inglese* (Milano, n.d.), pp. 168–9.

[2] Thus Tasso's pastoral drama *Aminta* must be mentioned in connexion, not only with *Comus*, but with *Lycidas* and the choruses of *Samson Agonistes*.

II

Important elements in Tasso's theory of epic diction were indicated in the last chapter, in the summary given of the dialogue *Il Tasso*.[1] But the detailed picture given by Tasso himself in his *Discorsi* introduces some new points which are no less essential; and it is worth surveying the whole matter as Tasso himself sees it, because this is the view in which it would first have appeared to Milton.

The three *Discorsi dell' Arte Poetica* were written in Tasso's youth and published in 1587; the *Discorsi del Poema Eroico*, published in 1594, were a revision and expansion of the earlier work. Tasso wrote the first set of *Discorsi* to prepare himself for the composition of the *Gerusalemme*; the second, while preserving an appearance of theoretic detachment, was intended to justify the epic he had produced. There can be little doubt that Milton had both sets in mind when he referred to Tasso's critical writings in the tractate *Of Education*.[2]

The chief purpose of the *Discorsi dell' Arte Poetica* is to distinguish epic poetry as the highest object of a poet's ambition, and they define Tasso's idea of heroic diction clearly enough for that purpose. 'There are three kinds of style,' he writes, 'magnificent or sublime, mediocre, and low. . . . The magnificent therefore suits epic poetry, as proper to it.'[3] And he continues: 'The heroic style is as it were midway between the simple gravity of tragedy and the flowery beauty of the lyric, and surpasses both in the splendour of a marvellous majesty.' Tasso also suggests briefly 'how this magnificence may be acquired' by means of suitable thoughts, words, and arrangements of words. But his advice is

---

[1] See pp. 19–24.   [2] See p. 70.
[3] Discorso Terzo (*Opere* (Pisa, 1823), xii. 234.)

here in general terms, and somewhat cautious: 'To transpose words sometimes, contrary to common usage, although rarely,' he suggests, 'may give nobility to the language.'

From these passages the fourth and fifth of the *Discorsi del Poema Eroico* develop a lengthy and intricate discussion of the 'magnificent' style. Here Tasso is determined to display all his learning in Greek and Latin rhetoric and poetry, and industriously accumulates commonplaces from ancient and modern grammarians. His critical analysis is full of the difficult terminology of his period, and illustrates also his own inveterate loquacity. Yet the stylistic theories he offers are in fact full of original perception, and he has many specific practical suggestions to give to fellow craftsmen. What is even more helpful is the care with which he gives quotations to show the precise effects he has in mind: his advice on 'how to make the style great' consists indeed very largely of such examples of effects to be admired and imitated. Assuming, as his contemporaries assumed, that the ideal of epic 'magnificence' was to be found in Virgil, and in less perfection in Homer, he undertakes to produce from Italian poets devices which can be turned to the service of that ideal. He shows how parallels to Virgilian complexity can be obtained in Italian, by drawing out the sentences, suspending the completion of the meaning, departing from the natural word-order, and applying metrical devices to slow down and stiffen the movement of the verse.

Tasso is really writing in self-defence, in order to justify the striking contrast in style between his own chivalrous epic and that of Ariosto. He wishes to make clear that the contrast is due to his adoption of a distinct ideal of style, and that any comparison must take this into account. Ariosto, for all his echoes of Greek and Latin poetry, had aimed in the *Orlando Furioso* at a smooth clarity of diction and presentation. The more disinterested of Tasso's commentators acknowledged that the two epics could not well be judged by the same standards. 'In my opinion', wrote Orazio Ariosto, 'all that will ever be said in comparing the diction and style of Tasso with those of Ariosto will be futile, and a reasoning fruitlessly in circles: for in this respect they have taken paths not only divergent, but almost opposite to each other: Ariosto having chosen to use the character or idea of style called "lucid" by Hermogenes, and Tasso having in his mind's eye the idea or form of the "magnificent" style'.[1] And the brief outline this critic gives of the 'great or magnificent' style will serve to indicate the guiding principles of Tasso's own portrait of it: magnificence, says Orazio Ariosto, 'if we are to believe Hermogenes, Demetrius, and Aristotle himself, requires thoughts or conceits . . . high and illustrious, sought out with care, elaborated, and almost, as it were, violent. . . . Its verse is not slack or soft, but has at first appearance a certain roughness. . . .'

The word *asprezza*, 'roughness', represents one of Tasso's overriding principles. The style he delineates aims at difficulty. Sense and metre have to be preserved; but all the devices of language and versification described by Tasso are intended to produce a certain difficulty, even an obscurity, in the sense, and an equivalent difficulty, even a roughness, in the sound.

Thus the first requisite Tasso gives for magnificence in 'elocution' is 'the length of the phrases and of the periods, or of the clauses, whichever we wish to call them'; and after giving his examples, he adds that 'in

[1] Quoted in Tasso, *Opere*, x. 244.

these verses another cause of greatness is the sense, which remains suspended for so long'.[1] The suspension of the meaning is a 'cause of greatness', he explains, 'because it is with the reader as with one who travels through solitudes, to whom the inn appears more distant as he sees the roads more deserted and un-frequented, but many stopping-places and resting-places make even a long journey seem short'.[2]

Difficulty, or roughness, in the sound of the verse is given a similar justification. Whether it is due to accumulated consonants, to the collision of open vowels which must be elided to give an acceptable rhythm, or to the collocation of open vowels which are given their full value—and Tasso offers examples of all these effects—*asprezza* 'is also a common cause of great-ness and of gravity', because such effects 'are like one who stumbles, walking through rough paths: but this roughness suggests I know not what magnificence and grandeur'.[3]

The combination of difficult, complex diction and a slow, suspended rhythm had been made in Italian by only one poet before Tasso—by Della Casa. Both the comparisons Tasso here uses to describe these effects were also applied by him in his only study of Della

[1] Translated extracts are from the Fifth Discourse, *Del Poema Eroico, Opere,* xii. 142–66.

[2] This comparison appears also in Tasso's lecture on Della Casa's Sonnet LIX (Della Casa, *Opere,* i. 339), where it is attributed to Dionysius of Halicarnassus.

[3] This comparison also appears in the lecture on Della Casa's Sonnet LIX, and is there attributed to Demetrius Phalerius. Tasso's examples of *asprezza* include the following:

    (i) *Ella si star pur come aspr' alpe all' aura* (for the heavy con-sonants).

    (ii) *Fu consumato, e 'n fiamma amorosa arse* (for the elision of the vowels).

    (iii) *Poi è Cleopatra lussuriosa* (for the gap between the open vowels).

Casa's verse, the brief lecture on Sonnet LIX. Della Casa is the poet under whose influence Tasso makes his choice of 'magnificent' devices from Tuscan verse. His own attempt to create a new diction for his Heroic Poem had been based upon his response to the strange and solemn music of Della Casa's sonnets. What he does in this part of the *Discorsi* is to analyse and defend the sources of that music. 'All these things', says Tasso of his various examples of *asprezza*, 'are usually doubtless the means of producing the same effects; because the smooth and equable style may be more pleasing and sweeter to the ear, but it has no place in magnificence; therefore it was much disliked by Monsignor Della Casa.' And he quotes from Della Casa's Sonnet to Sleep, to illustrate a method which the poet had made peculiarly his own. 'Verses which are broken up and enter into one another . . . make the style magnificent and great', says Tasso, and cites:

> *O sonno, o della queta umida ombrosa*
> *Notte placido figlio, o de' mortali*
> *Egri conforto, obblio dolce de' mali*
> *Sì gravi, onde è la vita aspra, e noiosa.*
> *Soccorri all' alma omai, che langue, e posa*
> *Non have, e queste membra stanche, e frali*
> *Solleva: a me ten vola, o sonno, e l'ali*
> *Tue brune, sovra me distendi, e posa.*[1]

The poem was often used to illustrate how Della Casa departed from Petrarch's style, 'discovering an unfamiliar manner, no less full of novelty than of

---

[1] Sonnet L: 'O sleep, O placid son of quiet moist shady Night, O comfort of sick mortals, sweet forgetfulness of those heavy woes, whence our life is harsh and wearisome:

'Succour my spirit now, which languishes and takes no rest, and relieve these tired and frail limbs: fly to me, O sleep, and stretch thy brown wings over me, and keep them there.'

majesty: placing the pauses always in the middle of the lines, and keeping the reader suspended in delight and wonder'.[1]

Compared with Tasso's advocacy of these rhythmic novelties, and his painstaking analysis of their technical basis, the rest of his treatise on diction may seem a trifle commonplace. Some of his minute observations are of more importance than they appear at first sight, as when he praises the resounding effect of double consonants in the rhymes in Tuscan poetry.[2] But much of this listing of figures of speech, tricks of syntax and arrangement, is of minor relevance. None of the tissue of artifice which Tasso depicts is alien to the highly wrought texture of *Paradise Lost*; but Milton could go elsewhere for such remarks as Tasso makes on allegory, epiphonema, personification, and other figures of speech.

Only one feature deserves to be emphasized by quotation, and that is the repeated defence of complex word-order. 'Antipallage likewise, which one may call the mutation of cases, can increase the magnificence of the expression', says Tasso. His assumptions concerning the aesthetic justification of such artificiality are merely those common to all Renaissance criticism: 'Certainly in the mutation of cases, the more we remove ourselves from the common usages, the more noble and sublime the style becomes.' But the particularity with which, once more, he illustrates the application of the principle, reveals the importance it had already assumed in his verse. He accumulates examples: 'And beginning the verse with oblique cases usually has the same

[1] Quoted from Della Casa, *Opere*, i. 247.
[2] See also Tasso's dialogue *La Cavalletta*. The full importance of these terminations comes out in connexion with the prosody of Milton's blank verse and of the choruses of *Samson Agonistes* (see pp. 53–54 and pp. 165–6).

effect in the expression, which one may call oblique or distorted, as in those verses

> *Del cibo, onde 'l signor mio sempre abbonda*
> *Lagrime, e doglia, il cor mio lasso nudrisco.'[1]*

He hurries through devices of this kind towards the end of his exposition: 'And the transposition of words, because it is removed from the common usage, as this:

> *Ch'i belli, onde mi struggo, occhi mi cela.[2]*

And the disturbing of the natural order, placing those before which should be placed after, as in this:

> *Per la nebbia entro de' miei duri sdegni.[3]*

And hyperbaton, which we may call distraction or inter-position, of which we have here an example:

> *Quel, che d'odore, e di color vincea*
> *L'odorifero, e lucido Oriente,*
> *Frutti, fiori, erbe e frondi, onde il Ponente*
> *D'ogni rara eccellenza il pregio avea,*
> *Dolce mio lauro.'[4]*

The *Discorsi del Poema Eroico* thus provide a remark-ably complete picture of Tasso's ideal of epic style; they give both general principles and a compendium of effects to be imitated. Milton could have found nowhere else so sustained a discussion and defence of the style he was to make his own. At the same time, Tasso's criticism cannot be fully understood, and the possi-bilities of the 'magnificent' style could not be confidently estimated, without recourse to the poems in which he attempted to realize it. The *Gerusalemme Liberata* and

---

[1] 'On the food, in which my lord always abounds, tears and grief, my heart, alas, I nourish.'

[2] 'That the beautiful (whence I destroy myself) eyes hides from me.'

[3] 'Through the cloud I enter of my hard disdains.'

[4] 'That which in odour and in hue vanquished the odoriferous and lucid East, fruits, flowers, grass and leaves, whence the West had the prize of every rare excellence, my sweet laurel.'

the *Sette Giornate del Mondo Creato* show clearly, when looked at in conjunction with the *Discorsi*, what Tasso had in mind. They would also provide many lessons, many hints of how to avoid failure and how to secure success, to any poet who, like Milton, was ambitious of attaining Tasso's ideal of 'magnificence'.

III

The manner of writing evolved by Tasso in the *Gerusalemme Liberata* was recognized by his contemporaries to be as novel as that which Della Casa had introduced into the sonnet and the *canzone*; but Tasso's poem roused, by virtue of its heroic pretensions, a controversy so massive that it almost overwhelmed both poet and poem.[1] The fury with which the poem was attacked and defended was mainly concentrated upon the substance, not upon the diction, of the epic. The metaphysics of the Heroic Poem—its purpose, morality, and decorum—had an especial attraction for Italian critics of the period. Fortunately they do not concern the present study.

The only contemporary critic who is worth quoting in the present connexion is Galileo.[2] He took no part in the public controversy, and did not write his comments in the interest of any critical dogma or policy. His notes are those of an exceptionally vigorous-minded young

[1] Begun in 1563, the *Gerusalemme Liberata* was finished in 1575. After revision, it was printed in 1581. As a result of its doubtful reception, Tasso rewrote it almost entirely. His new and inferior version, the *Gerusalemme Conquistata*, published in 1593, was unable to supplant the earlier poem.

[2] Galileo's *Considerazioni sulla Gerusalemme Liberata* remained in manuscript until 1793. They are reported to have been written when he was 26. The text is given in Tasso, *Opere*, xxiii.

man of letters, whose profound admiration of Ariosto serves him as a measure of what to expect from a poem of chivalry. His final estimate of Tasso's genius and style, placed at the head of his comments, takes the form of a well-known comparison, and illuminates not only the more verbal qualities of the poem in which we are interested, but also the workings of Tasso's imagination.

One defect is especially common in Tasso [he says] as a result of a great lack of invention and a poverty of ideas: it is that, as he is often short of matter, he is forced to proceed by piecing together ideas having no dependence on or connection with one another; whence his narrative appears to be more often like a picture in inlaid woodwork (*intarsiata*) than in oil colours. For inlaid work (*tarsie*) being a placing together of little pieces of diverse colours, which cannot be joined together or combined so smoothly that their edges do not remain sharp and harshly distinct (because of the difference in colour), necessarily makes the patterns dry and crude, without fullness or relief.[1]

This 'inlaid' style is exposed in all its weakness by Galileo's running commentary on the poem. He points with contempt to Tasso's inverted and contorted figures of speech, such as:

> Di Colei, che sua diva e madre face
> Quel vulgo del suo Dio nato e sepolto.[2]

Did you ever in your life see such a stiffness (*durezza*) as in these two lines, and such a suspension of the mind as is needed to rearrange the words, so that their sense and construction can be understood? But this great pedant clings to this anchor, that *verba transposita non mutant sensum*, and takes no account of the dangers; indeed, the greater the obscurity, the more beautiful the artifice appears in his eyes. And this is because his mind goes no further than to find the construction of the sentence, and

---

[1] Tasso, *Opere*, xxiii. 133.
[2] *Ger. Lib.*, Canto II, stanza 5. They may be translated as: 'Of her whom the [Christian] common people make their goddess, and make the mother of their God [who was] born and buried.'

he cannot believe that those things are not skilful, but the miserable strainings of people who are trying to do what they are not fitted to do; for anyone can speak obscurely, but very few with clarity.[1]

Galileo condemns also the lavish use Tasso made of the intricate rhetorical figures recommended in the *Discorsi*. 'Such conceits', he says, 'can be tolerated only on two conditions; the one, that they are carried out with the greatest skill, so that their charm surpasses their affectation; the other, that they are in a detached poem, a poem finished in itself, such as a sonnet or a madrigal, which is all of the same texture; but in a continued narration they have no place. . . .' For, he says, we may take pleasure in various 'figures' in a ballet or in a dancing-school; 'but on the other hand it would seem highly unsuitable if a gentleman on his way to church or to the law-courts were to change his pace every hundred yards or so by cutting one or two capers, leaping into the air, and then proceeding on his journey'.[2]

Galileo's sarcasm does less than justice, however, to the aesthetic unity of the *Gerusalemme Liberata*. If it is true that Tasso's poetry is an elaborate tissue of conceits, literary reminiscences, conscious combinations of emotional and verbal effects, one must nevertheless give him the credit of having sustained this manner with remarkable intensity. And the result of his having done so is a powerful incantatory atmosphere. The description of De Sanctis of Tasso's 'tinsel' gives a better impression of the total effect. It is, he says,

an artificial form of representation, where the interest lies not in the thing, but in the way of looking at it. In this case the form is not the thing, but the spirit, with its attitudes which are easily classified according to their external features, and which have

---

[1] Tasso, *Opere*, xxiii. 143.   [2] Ibid., p. 146.

become a manner or habit of representation, such as Petrarch-
ism or Marinism. Since what is proper to this manner is a brief
song, closed in itself, which has its value not only in the rest of
the sentence but in itself, there develops the element of song and
music, a sonorous emphasis, a constant and monotonous trumpet note, with fixed pauses, fixed flourishes, fixed repetitions, with
a certain overtone as of one who cries out instead of speaking—
there is an *Arma virumque cano* from beginning to end, a raised
and strained tone, as of one who finds himself in a state of chronic
exaltation.[1]

One cannot open Tasso's poem at any point without
feeling the justice of these observations; but they should
not be taken to mean that this type of poetry has no
appeal. Its charm, its brilliance, its solemnity may be
theatrical, may be specious; but Tasso's personal intensity of feeling animates and redeems this world of
artifice. Take, as an example, the description of the
Mass said by the Crusaders on the Mount of Olives
before their assault on Jerusalem:

> *Poscia in cima del colle ornan l'altare,*
> *Che di gran cena al sacerdote è mensa;*
> *E d'ambo i lati luminosa appare*
> *Sublime lampa in lucido oro accensa.*
> *Quivi altre spoglie, e pur dorate e care,*
> *Prende Guglielmo, e pria tacito pensa,*
> *Indi con chiaro suon la voce spiega,*
> *Sè stesso accusa, e Dio ringrazia e prega.*
>
> *Umili intorno ascoltano i primieri;*
> *Le viste i più lontani almen v'han fisse.*
> *Ma, poi che celebrò gli alti misteri*
> *Del puro sacrificio: Itene, ei disse;*
> *E in fronte alzando a i popoli guerrieri*
> *La man sacerdotal, li benedisse.*
> *Allor se 'n ritornâr le squadre pie*
> *Per le dianzi da lor calcate vie.*[2]

---

[1] *Storia della Letteratura Italiana* (Bari, 1925), ii. 169.
[2] *Ger. Lib.*, Canto XI, stanzas 14–15. 'Then on the summit of the

Such a passage as this, and the preceding description of the solemn procession of the Frankish army, chanting the *casta melodia soave* of the Litany, is bathed in the 'dim religious light' of a romantic sensibility: the picture may be indistinct, but it is golden.[1]

The *Gerusalemme Liberata* thus attempted to combine the matter and some of the procedures of the Italian epics of chivalry, with the 'magnificent' style based principally upon Virgil. The combination was an uneasy one, and it is not surprising that the poem betrays a sense of strain. The *ottava rima* was not a suitable form of verse for the desired effect of sustained stiffness, weight, and richness; its supreme virtues as a vehicle of narrative poetry were its swiftness and clarity, and the regularly renewed vivacity made possible by its final couplet. The intricacy and elaboration of Tasso's language destroy most of these qualities. Moreover, while he loses the advantages proper to the form, the style he desires cannot be developed fully within these limits. The stanza itself imposes a movement and a pattern which do not allow the sense to be 'variously drawn out from one verse into another'; and a complex word-order is not only structurally unnecessary (since the

hill they deck the altar, which is the table of the great supper for the priest; and on both sides appears shining a sublime lamp kindled in lucid gold. Here William dons other garb, and that too golden and precious, and at first silently meditates, then lifts his voice in clear tones, confesses himself guilty, and thanks and prays to God.

'All about the leaders hearken humbly; the most distant at least there fix their gaze. But, when he had celebrated the high mysteries of the pure sacrifice, Go, he said; and lifting his sacerdotal hand high over the embattled nations, blessed them. Then turned back the pious squadrons by those ways they had trodden before.'

[1] As an admirable comparison and contrast, one might take from Ariosto the description of the behaviour of Charlemagne, his pious prostrations and intercessions, the day before the battle which is to decide the fate of Paris, besieged by the Saracens (*Orlando Furioso*, Canto XIV).

stanza is held together by the rhymes) but becomes positively tiresome.

If, in spite of these weaknesses, Tasso's epic neverthe-less had, and has, poetic power, that is for reasons which may be too complex to be defined. One factor has already been indicated: the genuine ardour of Tasso's romantic temperament. Others are the very real vitality of the chivalrous epic at the Court of Ferrara, for which Tasso wrote his poem, and Tasso's own subjection to its power from his childhood. The *Gerusalemme Liberata* succeeds, not as an Heroic Poem (that critical abstraction of the century), but as a romance of chivalry: not because of its self-conscious neo-classical solemnity, but because that is redeemed by an underlying *naïveté* descended from medieval romance. The sustained grandeur would be worthless without the instinctive popular faith on which the poem builds.

This combination, this compromise, is well illus-trated by the passage describing God as He looks down from Heaven and sees the Crusaders approach-ing Jerusalem; these lines may also be quoted as a final illustration of the parallel compromise between the ideal of 'magnificence' in diction and the pattern of the *ottava rima*:

> *Sedea colà, dond' egli e buono e giusto*
> *Dà legge al tutto, e 'l tutto orna e produce*
> *Sovra i bassi confin del mondo angusto,*
> *Ove senso e ragion non si conduce;*
> *E de la eternità nel trono augusto*
> *Risplendea con tre lumi in una luce.*
> *Ha sotto i piedi il Fato e la Natura,*
> *Ministri umili, e il Moto e Chi 'l misura,*
>
> *E 'l Loco, e Quella che, qual fumo o polve,*
> *La gloria di qua giuso e l'oro e i regni,*

Come piace là su disperde e volve,
Nè, diva, cura i nostri umani sdegni.
Quivi ei così nel suo splendor s'involve,
Che v'abbaglian la vista anco i più degni:
D'intorno ha innumerabili immortali,
Disegualmente in lor letizia eguali.[1]

Here is the complex word-order, and the effort to
draw out the sentences which, in this case, overflow
the limits of the stanza. Obscurity, and empty or vague
words or phrases, accompany this effort. Individual
statements are made to appear as pointed, or ingenious,
as possible, but the whole series does not 'hang together'
logically (the fault indicated by Galileo's epithet 'inlaid'). The abrupt transition from one statement to
another is, however, in accord with Tasso's ideal of
asprezza, difficulty, or 'violence', in the total effect.
Asprezza is introduced assiduously into the sound of
the verses, the most obvious device for this purpose
being the repeated collocation of open vowels recommended in *Del Poema Eroico*.

IV

Even so inadequate an account of the *Gerusalemme
Liberata* as the above is enough to show that the poem

[1] *Ger. Lib.*, Canto IX, Stanzas 56–57. 'He sat there, whence he,
both good and just, gives laws to all things, and all things adorns and
produces above the low confines of the narrow world, where sense
and reason cannot travel; and from eternity on the august throne he
shone with three lights in one light. He has beneath his feet Nature
and Fate, his humble ministers, and what is moved and who measures it [Time], and Place, and Her who disperses and whirls like
smoke or dust, according as it pleases above, the glory of this earth
and gold and kingdoms, nor cares she, goddess, for our human pains
[Fortune]. Here he so wraps himself in his splendour that even the
most worthy there find their eyes dazzle: about him he has innumerable immortal spirits, unequally equal in their bliss.'

could be of but a limited value to Milton in his construction of an epic diction in English. When one reads Tasso's epic with Milton's diction in mind, one is struck by a constant affinity between the two poets in the details of the phraseology, and one has the same sense of the poet's deliberate effort, the raised pitch of his verse, which De Sanctis calls in Tasso 'the monotonous trumpet note'; but Tasso's lyrical conceits and the movement of the *ottava rima* (to which they are related) make a total impression very different from that made by Milton's blank verse. If we had only the *Discorsi del Poema Eroico*, the *Gerusalemme Liberata*, and *Paradise Lost*, we could indeed conclude that Milton's epic manner in blank verse had come nearer to the 'magnificent' style described by Tasso than Tasso's own manner in the *ottava rima*. But fortunately we have further evidence of the relationship between the two poets in Tasso's own long blank-verse poem, the *Sette Giornate del Mondo Creato*, written during his last years at Naples and Rome under the patronage of Manso.

Like his *Torrismondo*, Tasso's *Mondo Creato* is generally neglected, and, one must admit, with reason. The true genius of this romantic poet is to be found in the softer emotions and richer colours of the *Aminta* and the *Gerusalemme Liberata*, not in his assumption of the extreme gravity of tragedy or religious meditation. But the relative poetic failure of the *Mondo Creato* cannot diminish its value for the study of Milton's diction. Here Tasso was free from the constraints of rhyme and the requirements of chivalrous romance, which had not combined quite happily with the style he had sought (though they may have provided the real vitality of the poem he produced). Blank verse proved to be the form most capable of sustaining the 'magnificent' diction inspired by Virgil and Della Casa and delineated in the *Discorsi*. The eight thousand lines of the *Mondo Creato* employ to the full the functional devices of 'magnificence'; if we compare them with *Paradise Lost*, it appears clearly that Milton recreated in English a blank verse diction devised in Italy three generations before.

The basic principles of this blank verse diction were those which Milton was to make his own: 'the sense variously drawn out from one verse into another', and the distortion of the natural word-order. These two principles are of course interdependent; both can only assume their full importance in blank verse, where they provide the means of constructing the 'verse-paragraph'. This method of writing heroic blank verse had never yet been used as freely, consciously, and consistently in Italian as Tasso uses it in the *Mondo Creato*.

Leaving aside the use of blank verse for dramatic dialogue (where the dramatic form itself in part relieves the poet of the need for sustaining a formal unity in the language), there had been in Italy before Tasso two important examples of the use of blank verse in a long poem: Trissino's *L'Italia Liberata dai Goti* and Caro's translation of the *Aeneid*.[1] Trissino's model was the simplicity of Homer, but Voltaire observed that he imitated everything in Homer except his genius, and his verse is of an almost prosaic flatness. Caro's *Eneide* was, however, quite another matter. So brilliant a translation, or paraphrase, that it has remained ever since the best Italian version of Virgil, it attempted to reproduce as far as possible precisely that Virgilian

---

[1] *L'Italia Liberata dai Goti*, 1547–8; Caro's *Eneide*, completed in 1565–6, and published in 1581. For specimens of blank verse from these poems see Appendix A.

dignity and splendour which were the objects of Tasso's ambition.

Caro and Della Casa were contemporaries and friends, and there can be no doubt that Caro felt the ambition to transpose a Latin style into Italian which marked the poets of that generation and that circle.[1] He was especially commended for the skill with which he had imitated the Virgilian word-music.[2] But the conditions and nature of his work limited its usefulness as an exemplar. Begun, it is said, as the result of a wager, it was continued almost as an improvisation; and the mere fact that Caro had before his eyes the text of Virgil, and limited his ingenuity to finding a parallel to the specific passage at which he had arrived, meant that he had no need to devise consistent principles and methods. His poem might provide innumerable suggestions as to the possibilities of blank verse in Italian, but it could not provide a precise working formula for an original composition.

This was exactly what Tasso, in accordance with the somewhat pedantic tendency of his mind, provided and applied in the *Mondo Creato*. One cannot analyse any passage without perceiving that he is working to rigid principles. For example, Caro allows himself considerable liberty in the line-endings: many of his lines end in two unstressed syllables; they are what are called in Italian *sdruccioli*.[3] Tasso not only eschewed

[1] For an exchange of sonnets between Della Casa and Caro see Della Casa, *Opere*, i. 114–15.

[2] See p. 21.

[3] A whole paragraph in Book I is composed with these endings:

> *Come addivien sovente in un gran popolo,*
> *Allor che per discordia sì tumultua,*
> *E' imperversando va la plebe ignobile . . .*

and so on for fifteen lines. *L'Eneide, tradotta da Annibal Caro* (Firenze, 1914), p. 6.

this liberty, but in this matter he seems to have tried to impose, and on the whole succeeded in imposing, a rule of thumb of his own: he is determined that as many as possible of his lines shall end in words with double consonants before the last syllable. In this systematic search for *doppie* he is faithfully following the principles laid down in the fifth of the *Discorsi del Poema Eroico*, where he had written that 'beyond all other things which cause magnificence in Tuscan poetry is the sound or, so to speak, the clamour, of the double consonants, which strike the ear in the last place of the verse'.[1] He quoted an example from Petrarch:

> *Mentre, che 'l cor dagli amorosi ve*rmi
> *Fu consumato, e 'n fiamma amorosa a*rse,
> *Di vaga fera le vestigie spa*rse
> *Cercai per poggi solitari ed e*rmi . . .*[2]

His obsession with this effect appears elsewhere in his criticism,[3] and obtrudes itself everywhere in his heroic poetry, whether in rhyme or blank verse.[4] And in the blank verse of the *Mondo Creato* the effort to end the lines with this energetic, harsh, resonance is particularly evident: of the 664 lines of the *Giornata Prima*, 496 are made to conclude with words containing *doppie*.

While it is possible to argue that an optional verbal enrichment such as this, cannot be considered a structural feature of the verse, its practical value is obvious. Such systematic usages are what a poet needs to

[1] *Opere*, xii. 146.
[2] Petrarch, *Il Canzoniere*, ed. M. Scherillo (Milano, 1925), No. CCCIV.
[3] In *La Cavalletta*, for example.
[4] The blank verse of *Torrismondo* shows the same feature.

give unity of style to a long poem, especially a long poem written in a medium so flexible as blank verse.[1]

The value, therefore, of Tasso's blank verse to sub-sequent writers of *versi sciolti* in Italian and to a writer capable, like Milton, of adapting it to another lan-guage is that it is constructed by such systematic means as these. The 'magnificence', the *asprezza*, which have been accepted as the ideal of style, have been found to reside in certain verbal devices (as well as, of course, in certain processes of the imagination): a formula has been found. Tasso seeks *asprezza* by accumulations of consonants, not only in the line-endings, but through-out his verses: and he uses everywhere the collocation of open vowels recommended in the *Discorsi*, and which is so facile in Italian. An English poet cannot hope to make quite such an habitual use of this effect, but Milton's use of open vowels in *Paradise Lost* is an adaptation of this Italian practice; it is the distinguish-ing mark of Milton's blank verse prosody, and its pur-pose and effect can only be understood in connexion with his Italian studies.[2] Milton had evidently accepted Tasso's opinion, confirmed by his own ear, on the 'magnificence' to be derived from this form of *asprezza*; and within the limits imposed by his own language, he made it one of the stylistic principles of his verse.[3]

It is difficult to choose from so long a poem, written in so uniform, indeed so monotonous a manner, pas-sages which will especially illuminate the structural

[1] The relevance of Tasso's *doppie* to Milton's prosody is discussed below. See p. 135.

[2] Robert Bridges emphasized the inadequacy of the term 'elision' to describe Milton's treatment of open vowels in his mature blank verse (*Milton's Prosody* (Oxford, 1893), p. 49).

[3] See p. 133.

basis of the style. However, it is fair to choose passages in which the poet appears to be making a special effort; for the *Mondo Creato* is the work of an oldish poet, one who has suffered many afflictions, and whose tiredness and inability to concentrate his thoughts are often revealed in the writing. One may choose, then, the invocation to the Holy Spirit which occupies the first seventy-seven lines of the *Giornata Prima*:

> *divino Amore,*
> *Tu dal Padre, e del Figlio in me discendi,*
> *E nel mio core alberga, e quinci, e quindi*
> *Porta le grazie, e 'nspira i sensi e i carmi,*
> *Perch' io canti quel primo, alto lavoro,*
> *Ch'è da voi fatto, e fuor di voi risplende*
> *Meraviglioso; e 'l magistero adorno*
> *Di questo allor di voi creato mondo,*
> *In sei giorni distinto. O tu l'insegni . . .*
> *. . . Tu le cagioni a me del nuovo Mondo*
> *Rammenta omai, prima cagione eterna*
> *Delle cose create innanzi al giro*
> *De' secoli volubili, e correnti.*
> *E qual pria mosse te, cui nulla move,*
> *Motor superno, all' mirabil' opra,*
> *Già novissima esterna, omai vetusta,*
> *Che tutto aduna, e tutto accoglie 'n grembo . . .*[1]

[1] *Opere*, xxvii. 3. 'Divine Love, thou from the Father and the Son descend in me, and lodge in my heart and from the one and from the other bring me grace, and inspire my senses and my songs, that I may sing that first, exalted work, that was done by you, and now separated from you shines marvellously; and the fair governance of this world then by you created, divided into six days. O do thou teach it . . . do thou now recall to me the occasions of the new world, thou the first eternal occasion of created things, things created before the circle of whirling and unrolling centuries. And what too moved thee, thou whom nothing moves, thou supernal Mover, moved thee to the wondrous work, then lately brought. forth and now old, thou who gather'st all things and receiv'st all in thy bosom. . . .'

Another passage of exaltation is found in Tasso's vision of the Last Judgement in the *Giornata Settima*:

> *Là dispensate fian corone e palme*
> *A' gloriosi, e seggi alti lucenti.*
> *E quei, che guerreggiaro in lunga guerra,*
> *Quant' è la vita de' mortali erranti*
> *Sovra la terra, e riportar vincendo*
> *Dal nemico Satanno in duro campo*
> *Mille vittoriose e sacre spoglie;*
> *Lassù vedransi trionfando a schiera*
> *Nel gran trionfo eterno, e 'l gran vessillo*
> *Coronati seguir del Re possente*
> *Degli altri Regi. E la divina destra*
> *In quel d'eternità lucido tempio,*
> *Onde precipitando Angel rubello*
> *Cadde, sospenderà le spoglie eccelse,*
> *E i trofei della Croce.*[1]

Le Sette Giornate del Mondo Creato is not a great poem. Italian critics will no doubt continue to attribute its failure to the intellectual climate of the Counter-Reformation.[2] But, whatever the explanation, it is clear that Tasso had not at this time—perhaps he had not at any time—the power to wield the style he had evolved. The grandeur of manner and language is not matched by a true greatness of mind in the poet. His handling of the theme of the Creation is without system or clarity.

---

[1] *Opere*, xxvii. 269–70. 'There shall be distributed crowns and palms to those in glory, and high shining thrones. And those who warred in long-drawn war (for such is the life of wandering mortals on earth), and brought back conquering from their enemy Satan on the hard battlefield a thousand victorious and holy spoils; there above shall be seen triumphing in their ranks in the eternal triumph, and following crowned the great banner of the all-powerful King of Kings. And the right hand of God, in that shining temple of eternity whence cast down fell the rebel Angel, shall suspend the glorious spoils and trophies of the Cross.'

[2] De Sanctis, *Storia della Letteratura Italiana* (Bari, 1925), ii. 151.

Long and rich (though always vague and conventional) descriptions are mixed with moral platitudes
and undigested natural history. Tasso seems to have
wished to write as a Christian Lucretius, but his
would-be scientific survey of the Universe is mixed
with the prosy or quaint piety of medieval writers.
Certain birds are said in the *Giornata Quinta* to en-
gender without coition; and Tasso takes occasion to
reprove those who doubt the Virgin Birth. A few lines
later he mentions the silkworm, and exhorts those
ladies who embroider silken garments to remember
that our fleshly garment will rise incorrupt at the
Resurrection: a reflection which offers him a bridge
to a description of the birth, life, and death of the
Phoenix.[1] The fatal weakness of the poem is that both
the 'magnificent' diction and Tasso's lack of intellectual discipline lead him to say too much on every
subject. He may achieve passages of impressive splendour, but he usually blurs their effect by adding too
many connected reflections.[2]

Tasso's intellectual mediocrity is to be reckoned with
in any comparison of the relative failure of his heroic
blank verse with the undoubted success of Milton's.
But it has little to do with the technical aspects of his
style, in which is to be found the unmistakable model
of Milton's blank verse.

[1] *Opere*, xxvii. 202–6.
[2] Thus in the *Giornata Terza* he concludes the description of the
newly created sea with the following picture:

> Ma da qual alto, e 'n mar pendente scoglio
> E da qual più sublime eccelsa rupe;
> Da qual sommo di monte alpestre giogo,
> Che signoreggia d'ambe parti il mare,
> Vedrò la sua beltà sì chiaro e tanto,
> Quant' ella innanzi al suo Fattor s'offerse?

But he adds two lengthy pious glosses which dissipate the impression
(ibid., p. 79).

4

MILTON'S MINOR POEMS

I

WITH the exception of the mature sonnets and some of the translations of the Psalms, Milton's minor poems belong to the first thirty years of his life and represent for the most part a sustained effort of self-education in writing English verse. It is not impossible, however, to distinguish between those which are predominantly deliberate exercises in poetry and those which have drawn also upon deeper sources of inspiration. Thus *L'Allegro* and *Il Penseroso* and *Comus*—to take examples from the finest poems of this sort—are clearly written in what Keats called 'an artful or rather artist's humour'; while the hymn *On the Morning of Christ's Nativity* and *Lycidas* seem to mark, not only stages in Milton's acquisition of technical skill, but also important advances in imaginative power.

It is natural that, in a process of self-improvement such as the minor poems represent, the poet should produce some work of a kind which he does not repeat, and that much should appear which does not appear in quite the same guise in his later verse. So, to examine the minor poems in order to trace the ways in which Milton assimilated the Italian poetry he admired, is to find that many of them more obviously illustrate other things. If one considers Milton's English verse as a whole up to 1638, it shows that his chief purpose was to assimilate as much of the English poetic heritage as he found worthy and capable of being turned to his own use. The poetry of this period attempts less to ab-sorb Italian technique (except in a few important cases) than to plunder Shakespeare, Spenser, Fletcher, and Ben Jonson of treasures with which Milton could build a more lofty, polished, and condensed poetic style than had yet been achieved in English.

Spenser and Jonson are taken by Milton as his masters in the earliest English poems. The influence of Spenser prevails in the specifically religious pieces: *On the Death of a Fair Infant*, *On the Morning of Christ's Nativity*, and *The Passion*. Jonson's influence is stronger in the more secular or courtly: *At a Vacation Exercise*, *An Epitaph on the Marchioness of Winchester*, *On Shake-speare*, *On the University Carrier*. Milton's cultivation of English verse begins appropriately under the joint auspices of these two poets, for they alone among the great Elizabethans and Jacobeans held the lofty Renais-sance ideal of a learned poetry; and they alone upheld and applied critical theories which Milton could respect.

Milton's direct recourse to Italian poetry for tech-nical lessons is, however, apparent even among the first group of his youthful poems. It is possible to trace the workings of this idiosyncrasy and to distinguish the results from those of the more diffused Italian influence which comes through Spenser and his school. The hymn *On the Morning of Christ's Nativity* illustrates this reflection of Italian form in the Spenserian tradition; the lines *Upon the Circumcision* show that at the same time Milton was willing to go directly to Tuscan poetry; and the lines *On Time* and *At a Solemn Musick* show the interplay of the two influences: they could not have been written as they were without Italian exemplars, but they indicate that Milton will henceforth prefer to follow only those Italian lyric forms which he can modulate in his own way.

In all the early poems, except the early sonnets, the following of Italian verse affects the prosody rather than the diction. Indeed, Milton's adaptation of devices of Italian diction, which is all-important to the understanding of his mature verse, does not begin until *Lycidas*, the last poem of his youth.

II

A glance at the hymn *On the Morning of Christ's Nativity* will show that what Italianisms we find in these youthful poems may be ascribed almost wholly to Milton's following of Spenser. The Spenserian quality of the language and the rhythms of the hymn is a commonplace of criticism. It appears in nothing more clearly than in the management of adjectives; and such usages as 'dark foundations deep', 'flowre-inwov'n tresses torn', and 'Timbrel'd Anthems dark', which Spenser derived from the Italians, Milton accepts as proven elements in English poetic diction. The stanza itself reveals the same origins. The concluding alexandrine seals its Spenserian character, and both this and the preceding octosyllable would be impossible in any strict adherence to the methods of the Italian *canzone*. Yet the pattern and movement of the stanza, and the very notion of employing such a stanza for a solemn ode of this sort, could only derive from the tradition of the *canzone*. Spenser himself took similar liberties in the *Epithalamion* and the *Prothalamion*, which nevertheless remain his tribute to the power of the *canzone* form. Milton may well have considered that

such variations as alexandrines and octosyllables, as
well as occasional rhythms such as

> And then at last our bliss
> Full and perfect is,

were desirable in an English adaptation of Italian prosody. And perhaps he was right, and may have been
confirmed in his instinct by mature experience; for
there is reason to believe that the much greater licence
of the choruses of *Samson* represents his later version of
the rhythmic complexity of Italian verse.

The confidence of the hymn *On the Morning of
Christ's Nativity* is often contrasted with the relative
failure of two experiments which must have closely
followed it: the lines *Upon the Circumcision* and *The
Passion*. There can be little doubt that the young
Milton, fired by the sense of self-discovery and of poetic
power conferred by his celebration of the birth of
Christ, set out to hail in the same way those feasts of the
Church which recorded the chief events in the scheme
of Redemption. The poet's acceptance of defeat in this
plan came with his relinquishment of the poem on *The
Passion*, which has nothing to tell us of his technical
progress. But this unsuccessful experiment must have
been preceded in the New Year by the lines *Upon the
Circumcision*, which, within their narrow limits, provide interesting evidence of the poet's methods.

It has never yet been noticed that these two stanzas,
each of fourteen lines, reproduce as closely as possible
the stanza used by Petrarch in his *canzone* to the
Blessed Virgin. The only modification Milton makes,
and it is a modification only for the eye, is to make two
lines out of the two sections into which Petrarch's last
line falls. Petrarch's last line is linked to its predecessor
by *rimalmezzo* (medial rhyme); Milton follows the

rhyme-pattern, but changes the accepted Italian way of
setting out the verse, no doubt because he decided that it
would be unfamiliar and unpleasing to English readers.[1]
A comparison between the first stanzas of the two poems
makes the relationship clear and brings out other points.

Petrarch writes:

Vergine bella, che di Sol vestita,	a
Coronata di stelle, al sommo Sole	b
Piacesti sì che 'n te sua luce ascose;	c
Amor mi spinge a dir di te parole,	b
Ma non so 'ncominciar senza tu' aita	a
E di Colui ch'amando in te si pose.	c
Invoco lei che ben sempre rispose,	c
Chi la chiamò con fede.	d
Vergine, s'a mercede,	d
Miseria extrema de l'umane cose	c
Già mai ti volse, al mio prego t'inchina;	e
Soccorri a la mia guerra,	f
Bench'i' sia terra, — e tu del ciel regina.[2]	(f) e

And Milton:

Ye flaming Powers, and winged Warriours bright,	a
That erst with musick, and triumphant song	b
First heard by happy watchful Shepherds ear,	c
So sweetly sung your Joy the clouds along	b
Through the soft silence of the list'ning night;	a
Now mourn, and if sad share with us to bear	c
Your fiery essence can distill no tear,	c
Burn in your signs, and borrow	d
Seas wept from our deep sorrow,	d
He who with all Heav'ns heraldry whileare	c
Enter'd the world, now bleeds to give us ease;	e
Alas, how soon our sin	f
Sore doth begin	f
His Infancy to sease!	e

[1] The last two lines are written as one in the Trinity manuscript,
the reading of the printed text being proposed in a marginal cor-
rection.   [2] *Il Canzoniere* (Milano, 1925), No. CCCLXVI.

The lines *Upon the Circumcision* have the distinction of being Milton's only attempt to follow an Italian model in exactly this manner: that is to say, copying a complex stanza which must be repeated throughout the poem. Petrarch's *canzone* is 137 lines long; the fact that Milton, taking a stanza designed for a poem of this length, repeats it only once, may be a mere accident. There is nothing to indicate that his poem was intended to be longer than it is. But the brevity of the poem, and its unique fidelity to such a stanza-form, may well suggest that Milton's talent did not function easily on such a basis. The only stanza-form he continued to use was that of the sonnet, and then only in a manner which very considerably modified its stanzaic character.

The comparison between Milton's and Petrarch's stanzas shows also that Milton's are not articulated in the traditional manner. In the first stanza he does not observe the pause at the end of the sixth line which in Petrarch marks the end of the *fronte* of the stanza and the beginning of the *sirima* or *coda*.[1] Either Milton at this time had not appreciated the significance of these divisions (which had indeed been blurred in many *canzoni* of the sixteenth century), and when he came to do so, decided against the attempt to imitate such complexities in English: or he found the attempt in this poem uncongenial and unsuccessful, and forswore such metres for ever.

For the two other pieces of this period are indeed sufficiently Italianate, but they take as their basis an Italian form, the madrigal, which is less exacting than the *canzone*, and which Milton can develop with characteristic power. *On Time* and *At a Solemn Musick* have a sonority, a sustained emphasis of statement, and a rhythmic weight which give an assurance that

[1] See p. 84 for the significance of these terms.

Milton is again on the right track, finding means of expression which will bring out his full powers. *On Time*, which the Trinity manuscript tells us was conceived as an inscription for a clock-case, derives from a branch of Italian poetry much cultivated in the later sixteenth century by Tasso, Marino, and others: the madrigal, used to reproduce the Greek epigram. Like many of their originals, these madrigals drew their subjects from pictures or statues and preserved the link between epigram and inscription. Drummond of Hawthornden was the only poet writing in English who had closely imitated the madrigals and epigrams of Tasso and his followers; Milton was not likely to be impressed by his pedestrian versions of these witty trifles. Yet his own more ambitious use of the form follows its essential features. In both these poems he builds up a triumphant epigrammatic close, which is marked by an alexandrine; both have an element of 'wit-writing', though this is outweighed by a religious gravity and fervour.

The madrigal in its origin was as it were merely one stanza of a *canzone*—a stanza which was not repeated; and it shared with the *canzone* the metrical basis of hendecasyllables and heptasyllables which had proved useful in English verse. Milton preserves the general nature of the form, but modifies it significantly, not only in his concluding alexandrines, but in his handling of the shorter lines. The Italian heptasyllable had found its theoretic equivalent in English in a line of six syllables and three stresses. Milton experiments, not only with this accepted equivalent, but with lines of four stresses. These are slightly tentative in the lines *On Time*:

> With an individual kiss;

and

> Then all this Earthy grosnes quit,

but provide the first magnificent climax of the second poem:

> With those just Spirits that wear victorious Palms,
> Hymns devout and holy Psalms
> Singing everlastingly; (*At a Solemn Musick*, ll. 14–16.)

These modulations are indicative of a feeling on Milton's part that full sonority in these Italianate forms could not be attained by pedantic imitation, and that he for his part could achieve the effect he wanted rather by a certain disciplined improvisation. The significance of the two poems is increased when we notice how this disciplined improvisation has enabled Milton to develop the long and elaborate sentence which is to be a structural element in all his mature poetry. *At a Solemn Musick* in particular shows his resources:

> That we on Earth with undiscording voice
> May rightly answer that melodious noise;
> As once we did, till disproportion'd sin
> Jarr'd against natures chime, and with harsh din
> Broke the fair musick that all creatures made
> To their great Lord, whose love their motion sway'd
> In perfect Diapason, whilst they stood
> In first obedience, and their state of good.

The poet who can draw upon such a syntax and rhythm as this has little need of intricate rhyme or stanzaic form; at this point the poem slips into what we can scarcely call couplets, but what the Italians would call *rime baciate*, which are seldom used lavishly in Italian lyrics except as a sort of dizzy climax or conclusion (as in the *sonetto caudato*). The importance of *On Time* and *At a Solemn Musick* is that they point forward to *Lycidas* and the choruses of *Samson Agonistes*, and foreshadow Milton's exploitation of syntax as a structural element both in those later lyrics and in his blank verse.

In these youthful poems may be seen the deliberation with which Milton sets himself to learn what he needs from Italian verse. This deliberation is very marked also in his first sonnets, that is to say the Sonnet to the Nightingale, the sonnets in Italian, and the Sonnet on his twenty-third birthday. But these must be considered with the sonnets as a whole. Here it need only be re-marked that after this first phase of serious imitation of Italian verse Milton turns to English poetry and drama, and makes a thorough investigation of what they have to offer him.

III

The poems we associate with Milton's period of study at Horton display the results of this deliberate saturation in Elizabethan and Jacobean verse. Shake-speare, Jonson, and Fletcher are Milton's chief literary inspiration in *L'Allegro* and *Il Penseroso*; the titles are there to remind us of his special leaning towards Italian, but the metre and diction of these poems owe little to Italian verse, except perhaps a certain solidity and resonance which might equally well be attributed to Milton's cultivation of Latin.

Jonson is the presiding influence in *Arcades*, and determines the fundamental structure even of *Comus*, though *Comus* draws impressively on so many other sources. In its plan and in the texture of its verse *Comus* is based firmly on English masques and dramas; its relation to Italian pastoral drama, to Tasso's *Aminta* and Guarini's *Il Pastor Fido*, is indirect and subordinate. That Milton knew *Aminta* and *Il Pastor Fido* goes without saying; but his own poem owes more to Fletcher's *Faithful Shepherdess*, to Ben Jonson's masques and Shakespeare's plays, and to Spenser's blend of chivalry, pastoral and Renaissance philosophy.[1]

Comus is by virtue of its length and the variety of its verse one of the most important illustrations of Milton's art before his visit to Italy. In the blank verse dialogues there is much that remains apparent in his mature epic verse. But there is a distinction to be made between this blank verse and that of *Paradise Lost*, which may help to bring out the specifically Italian element in the latter. Dr. Johnson remarks in connexion with *Comus* that

Milton appears to have formed very early that system of diction, and mode of verse, which his maturer judgement approved, and from which he never endeavoured nor desired to deviate.

But the diction and the versification of the blank verse of *Comus* are not in fact identical with those of the great epics. Milton's feeling for the English language, the peculiar weight of his verse, these are of course fully present. We find his skill in constructing elaborate and extended verse paragraphs, and his delight in an over-whelming fullness of expression. Many passages convey a sense of discovery as well as achievement, a reaching out towards a new style:

> Within the navil of this hideous Wood,
> Immur'd in cypress shades a Sorcerer dwels
> Of *Bacchus* and of *Circe* born, great *Comus*,
> Deep skill'd in all his mothers witcheries,
> And here to every thirsty wanderer,
> By sly enticement gives his banefull cup,
> With many murmurs mixt, whose pleasing poison

[1] Professor Mario Praz exaggerates when he writes: 'Si è molto parlato del carattere spenseriano del *Comus*, ma nessuno sembra essersi accorto che il modello reale è l'*Aminta* del Tasso'. *Rapporti tra la letteratura italiana e la letteratura inglese* (Milano, n.d.), p. 169.

The visage quite transforms of him that drinks,
And the inglorious likenes of a beast
Fixes instead, unmoulding reasons mintage
Character'd in the face; this have I learn't
Tending my flocks hard by i' th hilly crofts,
That brow this bottom glade, whence night by night
He and his monstrous rout are heard to howl
Like stabl'd wolves, or tigers at their prey,
Doing abhorred rites to *Hecate*
In their obscured haunts of inmost bowres.

(*Comus*, ll. 520–36.)

This has Shakespeare's plenitude and weight, in-valuable in dramatic verse. But it has these qualities to excess, because Milton's prime purpose is not dramatic but literary, and he is working towards the creation of a style essentially unsuited to drama. 'It is a drama in the epick style, inelegantly splendid', says Dr. Johnson. Milton's special preoccupation here is clearly to extend the limits of the sentence, as he is to find means of doing, more appropriately, in his epic verse.

Yet it is worth observing that the wonderful elabora-tion of this blank verse style in *Comus* is achieved with-out making use of many of the devices of *Paradise Lost*. Astonishing periods are constructed almost entirely without the 'Miltonic inversions' to be derived later from Virgil and the Italian experiments in epic dic-tion. Lines and sequences of lines may be found almost everywhere which could occur also in the later blank verse; there is no consistent difference in the prosodic basis, though certain 'liberties' appear, both here and in the dialogues of *Samson Agonistes*, which suggest that Milton distinguished between dramatic blank verse and blank verse in narrative poetry. It would be difficult to demonstrate that the blank verse of *Comus* is a different metre from that of the epics. But it is sung to a different tune, as it were; it has a different movement and pitch; it has behind it a different pattern. *Paradise Lost* has the movement and tone of Virgil, and it has the pattern of Italian *versi sciolti* of the sixteenth century. *Comus* ob, serves the tone and movement of Shakespeare's blank verse, adapting also inflexions from lesser dramatists.

The lyrics of *Comus*, like those of *Arcades*, are related primarily to Jonson and Fletcher; if any affinities could be traced with contemporary Italian lyrics, they would probably be found to be due to the common musical tradition.

The importance of *Comus* for our study of the de, velopment of Milton's verse is that it illustrates copiously his relation to the Elizabethans and Jacobeans. It shows him consciously assimilating what he could of these native beauties. He had no Italian models in mind on this occasion; if he had had any idea of re, producing in English the special qualities of the Italian pastoral dramas, the result would assuredly have been very different from what we have.

IV

Lycidas follows *Comus* and immediately precedes Milton's Italian journey; its formal significance is worthy of separate treatment. After its composition Milton abandons the study and assimilation of English poetry which he undertook, among many other labours, in the Horton period. Henceforth his poetry is to be planned entirely under the influence of the two classical literatures and of Italian, the authority of which he considers equal to theirs. This settled view of his is reflected in the tractate *Of Education*, which he first printed in 1644, and which was written after his return from the Continent.

In this plan of a complete intellectual equipment, Italian is the only modern language to be set beside Greek, Latin, and Hebrew ('whereto it would be no impossibility to add the *Chaldey*, and the *Syrian* Dialect'). Italian and classical poetry are to be studied in the light of sixteenth-century Italian criticism and its classical sources, Aristotle and Horace. Milton's imaginary pupils would thus learn 'what the laws are of a true *Epic* Poem, what of a *Dramatic*, what of a *Lyric*, what Decorum is, which is the grand masterpiece to observe'. And they would thus know what to think of their native literature: 'Thus would make them soon perceive what despicable creatures our common Rimers and Playwriters be, and shew them, what religious, what glorious and magnificent use might be made of Poetry both in divine and humane things.'

This is where Milton stands at the end of his long experience of education and self-education; and from this point of view he conceives and finally carries out his mature work.

5

LYCIDAS

I

Lycidas is the most impressive of Milton's minor poems and one of the chief glories of English lyrical verse. Dr. Johnson's severity towards the pastoral convention of the poem has had little effect upon its reputation and its appeal, and has been sufficiently answered by criticism from the early nineteenth century to our own time. His denial of beauty to the verse may be felt to be equally a revelation of the sharp limits of his sensibility; but it is somewhat more difficult to rebut, since the structure of the verse is indeed peculiar. We are not likely to find that 'the diction is harsh, the rhymes uncertain, and the numbers unpleasing'. Yet the fact that the principles of structure of *Lycidas* have never been applied by later poets suggests that they have never been completely understood, however much the poem has been admired.

This, the last poem of Milton's youth, and the most perfect, in fact shows him as more conscious than ever before of the possibilities of moulding English verse by Italian methods. *Lycidas* cannot be dissected without a knowledge of the Italian poetry of the sixteenth century. But it must be said that there is no exact parallel in Italian literature to the pattern of Milton's poem; there is no single model to which we can point. The poem results from Milton's appreciation of several different kinds of Italian verse, and his application of

certain first principles to form a new combination of
familiar elements. And, indeed, how could it be
otherwise, if the poem was to be what it is, a unique
utterance wrung from the poet by the event and the
circumstances? Much of the power of *Lycidas* flows
from the impression it gives of being thus shaped by a
particular occasion; Milton's personal participation in
the poem gives it its greatest strength. This impression
is one with the form of the poem—a development of
the disciplined improvisation of the lines *On Time* and
At a Solemn Musick. Such a method of writing verse
must necessarily produce poems which have a unique
shape and movement.

It is possible nevertheless to detect the discipline
which guides such poems, and in *Lycidas* it is the
discipline of the *canzone*, as it was modified and adapted
in lyrics and eclogues of the *Cinquecento*.

Some aspects of this relationship are obvious enough.
W. P. Ker pointed out that 'you cannot fully understand . . . *Lycidas* without going back to Italy and the
theory and practice of the *canzone*', and insisted that the
whole tradition of solemn odes in English, from
Spenser's *Epithalamion* to the nineteenth century, rested
upon Dante's description of the *canzone* in the *De
Vulgari Eloquentia*, and in particular on his consecration
of the harmony between hendecasyllables and heptasyllables.[1] The combination of ten-syllable and six-
syllable lines in *Lycidas* of course represents that Italian
harmony, but the connexion with the tradition of the
canzona goes farther than that.

The wide deviations from the strict form of the
canzone are, however, the first thing to be noticed.
A *canzone* consisted of a complex, fully rhymed stanza
of some length, repeated several times and followed by a

[1] W. P. Ker, *Form and Style in Poetry* (London, 1928), pp. 162-5.

shorter concluding stanza, the *commiato*. *Lycidas* consists
of eleven 'verse-paragraphs' of lengths varying from ten
to thirty-three lines, closely but irregularly rhymed, and
including ten lines, scattered throughout, which do not
rhyme at all; the last verse-paragraph is of eight lines,
rhymed like an *ottava rima*, and undoubtedly corresponds in its own way to a *commiato*. The six-syllable
lines are disposed as irregularly as the rhymes, but are
governed nevertheless by certain limitations: they are
used somewhat sparingly, and they always rhyme, and
always with a ten-syllable line which has gone before.[1]

II

Milton must have been well acquainted with the
liberation of some Italian lyric verse from stanzaic form
which took place in the latter half of the sixteenth century and which had produced a great flow of facile
writing by his own time. There is no need to undertake the difficult task of tracing how this liberation
came about, for there can be little doubt that Milton's
first and clearest impression of it would have come
from two works, Tasso's *Aminta* and Guarini's *Il Pastor
Fido*. Tasso's famous pastoral drama must have established the use, for certain purposes, of such irregularly
rhymed passages, though it seems that his father
Bernardo had experimented with such forms in
eclogues and some other elaborate poems.[2] Guarini developed this feature of *Aminta* with great success;
among his choruses are to be found, together with the
normal use of regular *canzone* form, several examples of
a sustained improvised pattern of rhymes.[3] From this
type of irregular lyric, and from the partially rhymed

[1] In making this predominance of longer over shorter lines
Milton follows Dante's prescription for a 'tragic' *canzone*.

[2] See Francesco Flamini, *Il Cinquecento* (Milano, n.d.), p. 193.

[3] See the choruses which conclude Act II and Act III; the second

semi-lyrical passages of dialogue found both in _Aminta_ and _Il Pastor Fido_, Milton would have seen the possibilities of this liberation of the _canzone_ for dramatic and lyrical verse. These pastoral dramas were among the most brilliant and most admired works of Italian poetry in the late sixteenth and early seventeenth centuries. Their artistic authority would certainly have been acknowledged even by a poet of so different a temper as Milton.

Nevertheless, the technical innovations of _Aminta_ and _Il Pastor Fido_ do not in themselves account for the structure of _Lycidas_, though they may help to explain how Milton arrived at his own methods. For with _Aminta_ the Italian pastoral began to move away from its dependence on Virgil's example, and entered a new world of its own, preoccupied with the affairs of the Amaryllis and the Naeara who are allotted two lines in Milton's poem. As Italian pastoral poetry became less learned and more facile it became less evocative of any associations other than erotic. _Lycidas_, with its repeated invocations of the 'Sicilian Muse', intends to remain within reach and touch of Theocritus and Virgil; and this intention it shares with the Italian eclogues of the earlier sixteenth century rather than with those of the later. The seriousness of the poem, however personal its intensity may be, is a quality it shares with the even earlier Latin pastoral tradition; in Italy, as the sixteenth century ran its course, such allusions as those of Milton to the Church became impossible.

Lycidas therefore takes advantage of the technical freedom of the later _Cinquecento_; but it uses that freedom in ways which recall also the Italian eclogues of

of these is given in Appendix B, p. 178. The use of the chorus by Tasso and Guarini must be discussed more fully in connexion with _Samson Agonistes_.

the High Renaissance, when vernacular poetry was
absorbed in its imitation of Greek and Latin.

III

The Italian eclogues of Sannazaro (1458–1530) and
Berardino Rota (1509–75) illustrate some of the tech‑
nical developments by which it was sought to recreate
Greek and Roman pastoral verse in traditional Tuscan
forms. The chief distinction between the methods of
these two poets is that by Rota's time the diction of
Italian verse had learned how to reproduce the move‑
ment of Latin syntax, and this made possible a freer
handling of verse‑forms.

Sannazaro's eclogues in Italian are interspersed
throughout his pastoral romance, the *Arcadia*; the more
lyrical of them preserve the fixed forms of the *canzone*
(including the *sestina*), but for the purposes of dialogue
Sannazaro uses *terza rima*, the form which was always
favoured for colloquial or familiar verse.[1] The mixture
of metres in individual eclogues, and the use of various
elaborate lyric forms, show the problems facing Italian
poets when they set out consciously to rival classical
pastorals. There was no single vernacular metre which
could be made the equivalent of the Virgilian hexa‑
meter, moving from dialogue to song without any
change of structure.

Sannazaro does not attempt any profound modifica‑
tion of the movement of the *canzone* in the elegy which
forms his Fifth Eclogue; he is content to infuse into
the diction as much as he can of the elegiac fluidity

---

[1] *Terza rima* continued to be used for pastoral eclogues through‑
out the sixteenth century; it is to be found in eclogues by Chiabrera,
who died in 1638, and who was admired by some of Milton's
Italian friends, if not by Milton himself. See *The Works of John
Milton* (New York, 1936), xii. 301.

and fullness already introduced by Petrarch in echo of Latin verse:

> *Altri monti, altri piani,*
> *Altri boschetti, e rivi*
> *Vedi nel cielo, e più novelli fiori;*
> *Altri Fauni, e Silvani*
> *Per luoghi dolci estivi*
> *Seguir le Ninfe in più felici amori,*[1]

sings Ergasto to the shade of Androgeo. And a passage which points forward to *Lycidas* describes the grief of Nature:

> *Pianser le sante Dive*
> *La tua spietata morte;*
> *I fiumi il sanno, e le spelunche, e i faggi:*
> *Pianser le verdi rive,*
> *L'erbe pallide e smorte;*
> *E 'l Sol più giorni non mostrò suoi raggi:*
> *Nè gli animai selvaggi*
> *Usciro in alcun prato;*
> *Nè greggi andar' per monti,*
> *Nè gustaro erbe, o fonti:*
> *Tanto dolse a ciascun l'acerbo fato;*
> *'Androgèo, Androgèo' sonava il bosco.*[2]

The diction and the placing of the words here are no more complex than in Petrarch; but they are more consciously used, as they are used also by Milton, to reproduce specific Latin effects.

[1] 'Other mountains, other plains, other thickets and banks, thou view'st in Heaven, and yet fresher flowers: other Fauns and other Silvans throughout sweet summer places follow the Nymphs in happier loves.'

[2] 'The holy Goddesses wept for thy despiteful death; the rivers know it, and the caves and beeches: the green banks wept, their grasses pale and withered; and the sun for many days concealed his rays: nor did the wild beasts come forth in the meadows, nor the flocks go to the mountains, nor tasted they grass nor fountain: so greatly each was grieved by thy bitter fate; "Androgeo, Androgeo" the wood resounded.'

The same modulation of the flow of the sentences is to be seen in some of Sannazaro's *terzetti*:

> *Talor mentre fra me piango, e ragionomi*
> *Sento la lira dir con voci querule:*
> *'Di lauro, o Meliseo, più non coronomi.'*
> *Talor veggio venir frisoni, e merule*
> *Ad un mio roscigniuol, che stride, e vocita:*
> *'Voi meco, o mirti, e voi piangete, o ferule.'*
> *Talor d'un alta rupe il corbo crocita:*
> *'Absorbere a tal duol il mar devrebbesi,*
> *Ischia, Capri, Ateneo, Miseno, e Procita.' . . .*[1]

The double rhymes of these lines are characteristic of Sannazaro's *terza rima*: their effect is to give the dialogue a sustained cleverness and a monotony of rhythm, which are both somewhat irritating. Such verse has a certain charm, and a flavour of common speech; but it is more suited to humorous writing than to serious, and Sannazaro on the whole uses it for such lighter passages as this exchange of abuse between rival shepherds:

OFELIA. *Dimmi, caprar novello, e non t'irascere,*
    Questa tua greggia, ch'è cotanto strania,
    Chi te la diè sì follemente a pascere?

ELENCO. *Dimmi, bifolco antico, e quale insania*
    Ti risospinse a spezzar l'arco a Clonico,
    Ponendo fra' pastor tanta zizzania?

OFELIA. *Forse fu allor, ch'io vidi malinconico*
    Selvaggio andar per la sampogna, e i naccari,
    Che gl'involasti tu, perverso erronico.[2]

[1] 'Sometimes while to myself I weep and talk, I hear the lyre that says with querulous tones: "O Meliseo, I crown me no more with laurel." Sometimes I see finches and blackbirds come to a nightingale of mine, that cries and calls out: "O myrtles, weep with me, and weep, ye fennels." Sometimes from a high rock the raven croaks: "At such a sorrow the sea should swallow Ischia, Capri, Ateneo, Miseno and Procita." '

[2] *Ofelia.* 'Tell me, new goatherd, and be not angry: this flock of thine, that is so odd, who gave it thee so foolishly to graze?'
Elenco. 'Tell me, old ox-driver, and what madness impelled thee

This jocular intricacy of surface betrays an inner emptiness. But Milton had a leaning towards this verbal type of humour. His sardonic sonnets on the reception of his divorce tracts and on the Long Parliament have roots in this kind of satire in Italian. There is surely an echo of this manner of rustic raillery in the description of the singing of the bad shepherds in *Lycidas*:

> And when they list, their lean and flashy songs
> Grate on their scrannel Pipes of wretched straw.
>   (*Lycidas*, ll. 123–4.)

The eclogues of the *Arcadia* display a balance between traditional Tuscan forms and the sustained imitation of Virgil's diction and manner. This balance is upset in the Italian eclogues of Berardino Rota, written some forty years later. The form and diction of these *Egloghe Pescatorie* show what progress Bembo and his disciples had made towards a close imitation of Latin verse in the vernacular. Rota was a younger contemporary of Della Casa, and the latinization of the style in his eclogues recalls Della Casa's infusion of Horatian and Virgilian gravity into the sonnet, and probably owes something to Della Casa's methods.

Neither in Rota's sonnets nor in his eclogues do we find any vivid or concentrated poetic power; but the very conventionality of his matter deflects attention to the small innovations of manner and method which give his eclogues their distinction. Himself a Neapolitan, he imitates and develops in the vernacular the

to break the bow with Clonico, so setting such discord among shepherds?'
Ofelia. 'Perhaps it was then when I saw Selvaggio go sadly lacking his pipe and castanets, which thou robbedst him of, thou wicked stray.'

Latin Piscatory Eclogues of Sannazaro. As Virgil invokes the Sicilian Muses, Rota invokes the Nymphs
of Mergellina; he derives as much from Sannazaro as
from Theocritus and Virgil.

His chief effort is directed towards making a new
adjustment between Italian verse-forms and Latinate
diction; the result is that the still surviving predominance of the rhymed patterns found in Sannazaro is here
replaced by the predominance of diction as an element
of structure. Intricate word-order, carefully sustained
repetitions, and lengthy periods tend to relegate rhyme
to a secondary position. Such writing is relevant, in
however minor a degree, not only to *Lycidas*, but to
Milton's blank verse.

In most of the lyrical parts of his eclogues Rota continues to use stanzaic forms; but for dramatic and
descriptive dialogue, and for some lyrics, he devises a
new formula. His hendecasyllables are built on a submerged pattern of six-line stanzas: a b c a b c e f g e f g,
and so on. The use of *terza rima* in pastoral verse is perhaps reflected in the ternary structure of this pattern;
but Rota succeeds in eliminating the strongly stanzaic
movement of *terza rima* by spacing his rhymes as widely
as he does. Moreover, the sense and the diction so
habitually disregard the limits of the lines and the
'stanza', they seem to observe but really transgress
the rhyme-scheme with such consistency, that there is
little difference in the effect when, as in the Second
Eclogue, submerged rhyme is abandoned for blank
verse.

The only satisfactory way to read Rota's rhymed
hendecasyllables is indeed as if they were *versi sciolti*; the
diction is elaborated in such a way as to impose its own
movement on the metre. The following passage from
the Eleventh Eclogue will illustrate this effect; Triton

sings of various fables of the sea, *a guisa del Sileno di Virgilio*:

A questo aggiunge poi perchè nell' acque	a
Ino col suo figliuol già si sommerse;	b
Come le fu cangiato, il viso, il nome	c
Dal Re del mar: che così a Vener piacque,	a
E in questo e quel Dio poi li converse;	b
E quanto pianta fu la Nimpha, e come	c
Giunone irata le compagne sue	d
Augelli e sassi fece. E di te disse	e
O Scilla ancor, qual fur dannose e vane	f
Le prighiere di Glauco; e quanto fue	d
Circe crudele, e'n quanto duol poi visse	e
L'amante, quando in mar rabbioso cane	f
Latrar t'intese a torto, e poichè scoglio	h
Ti vide, quanto pianse e quanto ancora	i
Ogni nocchier ti fugga, e perchè festi,	j
Rimembrando di Circe il fiero orgoglio,	h
Senza compagni Ulisse. E come fora	i
O Vener bella tu dal mar sorgesti	j
Nata di spume: onde 'l bel nome hai preso.[1]	k

Yet, for all its careful modulations, there is something mechanical about such verse. Rota has fluency, but little energy, and this is perhaps why he clings to a regular scheme of rhyme, when blank verse would seem to be the logical development of his style. His formula

[1] 'To this he adds then why Ino with her son was dipped in the waters; how she had her face and name changed by the King of the sea, for so it pleased Venus, and into this and that God then he changed them; and how much bewept was the Nymph, and how angry Juno made her companions stones and birds. And of thee he said, O Scilla, again, how harmful and vain were the prayers of Glaucus; and how cruel Circe was, and in what pain then lived thy lover, when he heard thee bark in the sea as a raging dog, and when he saw thee as a rock, how much he wept and how yet every sailor flees thee; and why thou deprivedst Ulysses of his comrades, remembering the fierce pride of Circe. And how it was that thou, O lovely Venus, rose from the sea, born of foam, whence thy fair name is taken.' *Egloghe Pescatorie del Sig. Berardino Rota* (Napoli, 1560), pp. 33*v.*–34.

is a compromise, and the opposition between the repeated pattern of rhymes and the irregular current of
the diction is too constant to be satisfying: it leaves a
faint impression of artistic dishonesty or cowardice.
Rota's methods point the way to Tasso's *Aminta*, in so
far as his eclogues suggest that blank verse, on the one
hand, or a greater freedom of rhyme on the other, would
open up new possibilities; Tasso's 'eclogue' combines
these more logical methods.

A knowledge of Sannazaro's and of Rota's eclogues
enables one to distinguish the main factors in the development of Italian pastoral poetry in the sixteenth
century. Taken together with *Aminta* and *Il Pastor
Fido*, they point to the underlying compulsions of
Milton's 'monody', why it seeks, and how it achieves,
a reconciliation between rhyme and fluent elegiac diction. *Lycidas* is more powerful than any of these elegant
literary amusements; but without the technical discoveries they represent Milton would have been unable
to give his pastoral its combination of freedom and
discipline.

IV

Two technical experiments—the attempt to evolve a
poetic diction equivalent to that of Virgil, and the
attempt to combine the tradition of the *canzone* with
that of the Classical eclogue—marked Italian pastoral
verse in the sixteenth century. In England both these
experiments bore fruit in *Lycidas*. But before considering Milton's poem more closely, it is worth looking at
the degree to which these Italian experiments are traceable in earlier English pastoral poetry. The only previous English poet worth considering in this connexion
is Spenser, the only poet to show, in *The Shepheardes
Calender*, that he believed the pastoral to be capable of

'high seriousness'. The general Elizabethan and Jacobean notions of pastoral, however delightfully they might enrich plays and lyrics, or narrative and topographical verse, were too popular and superficial to affect Milton's poem.

Spenser's methods in _The Shepheardes Calender_ are akin to those of the earlier type of Italian eclogue written by Sannazaro rather than to those tried out by Rota. Roughly speaking, we may say that he is not interested in the problem of metrical unity of effect that began to interest Rota and was solved by Tasso. Writing in stanzas (except in the three 'Chaucerian' eclogues), Spenser either preserves the same stanza throughout or introduces songs or 'layes' in different measures. The only reflection of _canzone_ form in _The Shepheardes Calender_ is in the dirge in _November_, and this, though of some interest in relation to Milton, has no prosodic affinity with _Lycidas_.[1]

It seems clear that Spenser's technique in pastoral verse was formed without reference to the particular Italian technical advances summarized above. This is confirmed by the form of his later pastorals, _Colin Clout's Come Home Againe_, _Daphnaïda_, and _Astrophel_. _Colin Clout_ indeed uses a metre not found in _The Shepheardes Calender_, continuous 'heroic' quatrains; and the way in which Spenser handles these, so that the limits of the quatrains have little correspondence with the flow of the verse, is faintly suggestive of Rota's device of submerged rhyme. But the analogy is slight because, for one thing, Spenser's quatrains are a shorter and more emphatic pattern than Rota's pattern of six lines and are more difficult to submerge; and for another, Spenser seems to make no effort to submerge them. He does not attempt, by means of a complex

---

[1] For a further reference to the Dirge for Dido see p. 163.

word-order or of strong pauses within the lines, to disguise the rhyme-scheme, but rather proceeds with his
usual mellifluous facility and produces an effect of his
own. There is, moreover, an English parallel to the
verse of *Colin Clout*, and that is the verse of Raleigh's
surviving fragment of *The Book of the Ocean to Cynthia*.
Since the two poets were closely associated at about this
time, and Spenser alludes to Raleigh's poetry in *Colin
Clout*, it is possible that the quatrains of this poem were
suggested by Raleigh's lost poem *Cynthia*, which may
have been in the same metre as the later fragment.

Daphnaïda and *Astrophel* were the finest pastoral elegies written in English before *Lycidas*, and must be
reckoned important features of Milton's poetic background. Yet in these later and more lengthy poems
Spenser does but apply the verse technique he had devised more than a decade before: here, as in the bulk
of his poetry, the characteristic rhetoric and music are
due to his genius for writing in stanzas. Milton had not
attempted to write in stanzas of Spenserian type since
he relinquished his poem on *The Passion*; what else
Daphnaïda had to give him—an example of flowing
melody—he must have appropriated long before composing *Lycidas*. The chief interest of a comparison between Spenser's pastoral elegies and Milton's would
consist in their divergences: Spenser's regularly woven
patterns and leisurely embroidery make an instructive
contrast to Milton's more compressed and more
passionate variety of movement.[1]

---

[1] Two of the elegies put together with Spenser's *Astrophel* show
that Spenser and his friends were by this time acquainted with the
newer forms of Italian pastoral: *The Mourning Muse of Thestylis* and
A Pastorall Aeglogue upon the Death of Sir Phillip Sidney Knight, etc.
Both are written in continuous but irregularly placed rhyme; the
second shows also an attempt to obtain Virgilian movement by
strong pauses within the lines.

V

It remains to show what specific means Milton employed 'to build the lofty rhyme'. The final clue to the structure of *Lycidas* is to be found in principles derived from the architecture of the *canzone*.

The structure of the *canzone* was fully explained by Dante in the *De Vulgari Eloquentia*; Tasso also discusses it in his dialogue *La Cavalletta*, and claims to discover some discrepancy between Dante's theory and his practice. But the principle of structure which is relevant to *Lycidas* is never in dispute: it is that the stanza of a *canzone* is most commonly built of two sections, which are linked by a key line or *chiave*. Such a stanza was also called a *stanza divisa*. One or the other of the two parts of such a stanza might also be divided, but not usually both. If the first part was undivided it was called the *fronte* or brow; if it was divided the subdivisions were called *piedi* or feet. If the second part of the stanza were undivided it was called the *sirima* or *coda*; if divided, the subdivisions were called *versi*. The first part of a *stanza divisa* must be linked to the second by a line rhyming with the last line of the first; this line was the *chiave* or key. The two *versi*, where these existed, might also be linked by a *chiave*.

It is the sense of movement, and the habits of rhetoric, deriving from these divisions, which determine the methods of Milton's poem. Just as in the original use of the sonnet the divisions and subdivisions between quatrains and tercets were observed by the diction and only transgressed for some special purpose, these divisions in the *canzone* were present to the writer and the reader and gave a distinctive emphasis and movement to the different parts of the stanza. And just as with the divisions of the sonnet, the divisions of the *canzone* were often deliberately overridden by sixteenth-century poets, but only because, even when the diction did not follow them, they remained in mind, and the effect was one of counterpoint between the rhyme-pattern and the diction, such as Milton reproduces in his sonnets. The divisions in both sonnet and *canzone* made possible a kind of rhetoric of rhyme: lines which rhymed had differing weight and emphasis according to their position and function. It is impossible to follow Milton's methods in *Lycidas* without perceiving that he makes use of such a rhetoric of rhyme, combining it and contrasting it with the more usual rhetoric of sentence-structure.

The most obvious feature which this method gives the poem is the failure of Milton's sentences to correspond to the pattern of rhymes; the ebb and flow of statement, the pauses and new departures, appear to be independent of any necessity but their own. To give two examples:

Next *Camus*, reverend Sire, went footing slow,	a
His Mantle hairy, and his Bonnet sedge,	b
Inwrought with figures dim, and on the edge	b
Like to that sanguine flower inscrib'd with woe.	a
Ah; who hath reft (quoth he) my dearest pledge?	b
Last came, and last did go,	a
The Pilot of the *Galilean* lake,	c

(*Lycidas*, ll. 103–9.)

Weep no more, woful Shepherds weep no more,	a
For *Lycidas* your sorrow is not dead,	b
Sunk though he be beneath the watry floar,	a
So sinks the day-star in the Ocean bed,	b
And yet anon repairs his drooping head,	b
And tricks his beams, and with new spangled Ore,	a
Flames in the forehead of the morning sky:	c

(*Lycidas*, ll. 165–71.)

In the first of these passages there is a strong pause at
the end of the fifth line, yet the next line, introducing a
new series of rhymes, takes its own rhyme from those
of the completed statement; in the second passage the
first strong pause comes at the end of the seventh line,
yet this line introduces a new rhyme. Everywhere in
the poem we find such effects, and they are due to the
working of a positive principle, not to a mere negative
overriding of a casual rhyme-scheme. Milton has in
mind the chief principle resulting from the *stanza divisa*
of the *canzone*: that each new group or series of rhymes
must be linked to its predecessor by a key line. In the
first example given, either the fifth or sixth line (but
preferably the latter) may be regarded as such a key,
taking up a rhyme from the first four lines. In the
second example the fifth line is such a key, though
again it is followed by a line which also takes up a
rhyme from the first four lines. A clearer example is
the fifth line of the following paragraph:

Return *Alpheus*, the dread voice is past,	a
That shrunk thy streams; Return *Sicilian* Muse,	b
And call the Vales, and bid them hither cast	a
Their Bels, and Flourets of a thousand hues.	b
Ye valleys low where the milde whispers use,	b
Of shades and wanton winds, and gushing brooks,	c

(Lycidas, ll. 132–7.)

Milton is using the principle of articulation of the
canzone; and he has liberated it from its association with
repeated *piedi* or *versi* within his paragraphs. This principle of articulation is therefore free to affect any part
of his paragraphs, not only certain transitions, like the
volta or, as Dante calls it, the 'diesis'.

The rhetoric of rhyme derived from the *canzone* has
thus provided Milton with an invaluable instrument—
a type of rhyme which looks both back and forward.

His ear had been so trained by the *canzone* as to appreciate this effect not only in the key, or *chiave*, where it is most obvious, but in subtler details. One of these is the use of the six-syllable lines, which are also placed so as to give a sense of expectation: they not only always rhyme with a previous longer line (thus looking back), but they give the impression of a contracted movement which must be compensated by a full movement in the next line (which is always of full length), and they thus look forward. This effect is most marked when, as in most cases, these short lines rhyme with the line immediately preceding them.

Milton has constructed *Lycidas* by means of these very precise principles, though they are principles which not only allow him a certain freedom of improvisation but even facilitate it, in a way that would be impossible if the verse were not closely controlled. He has made his own rules for this poem, but made them out of his knowledge and enjoyment of the strictest Italian practice. Thus he appears to have decided that his rhymes must not generally be separated by more than two lines.[1] For the scattered unrhymed lines he had sufficient Renaissance authority.[2] He has also accepted from Dante the preference for a couplet to end his paragraphs; according to the *De Vulgari Eloquentia*, 'the endings of the last lines are most beautifully disposed if they fall with a rhyme into silence'.

Indeed, the only true couplets in *Lycidas* are those which conclude verse-paragraphs; and one of the best

[1] In ll. 64 and 70 the rhyme is separated by four lines; in ll. 98 and 102 by three.

[2] Even in the earlier, stricter, form of the *canzone* unrhymed lines could occur in fixed positions, as in Dante's *canzone* 'Lo doloroso amor che mi conduce'. *Le Opere*, No. XVI*, ed. E. Moore and Paget Toynbee (Oxford, 1894).

ways to appreciate the articulation of the poem is to
analyse the effect of those rhymes coming together elsewhere, which might appear to be couplets, but which
are not, because the second rhyming line always looks
forward to what comes next. The following examples
illustrate this effect in varying degrees:

Begin then, Sisters of the sacred well,	a
That from beneath the seat of *Jove* doth spring,	b
Begin, and somwhat loudly sweep the string.	b
Hence with denial vain, and coy excuse,	c
It was that fatall and perfidious Bark	a
Built in th' eclipse, and rigg'd with curses dark,	a
That sunk so low that sacred head of thine.	b
Fame is no plant that grows on mortal soil,	a
Nor in the glistering foil	a
Set off to th' world, nor in broad rumour lies,	b
But lives and spreds aloft by those pure eyes,	b
And perfect witnes of all judging *Jove*;	c

To analyse *Lycidas* in the light of the *canzone* and the
Italian eclogues is to realize with vividness that only a
poet of Milton's intellectual energy could have devised
and successfully applied such a formula. The poem is
built upon movements of thought and emotion; Milton
is able to use the methods of repeated transitions, of a
continuous unfolding and developing, because his
mind and emotions naturally moved with power and
confidence, with a sustained strength. Even when other
poets who have attempted solemn odes in English have
had some of this capacity for embodying mental and
emotional energy in verse, they have lacked a technical
formula so appropriate to such a task. The discipline of
Lycidas has left little mark on the tradition of the English
ode; it has proved to be inimitable. And this is scarcely
surprising, if the peculiarly combined forces described in
this chapter are among those which went to its making.

6

MILTON'S SONNETS

I

THE 'Petrarchian stanza', as Milton calls it,[1] is the only fixed form from Italian poetry which he continued to use after the early experiment of the lines *Upon the Circumcision*. His style developed, and was to produce its most ambitious structures, under the influence of Italian forms. Yet he takes from Italian verse only such principles as he can apply with considerable freedom: the disciplined improvisation which he discovers to be his bent transcends recurrent metrical patterns. He was able to remain faithful to the fixed pattern of the sonnet only because the particular tradition of Italian sonnet-writing he followed allowed a deliberate modification of its stanzaic character.

J. S. Smart's edition of the sonnets placed them clearly both in relation to the sixteenth-century Italian tradition and in relation to the rest of Milton's verse. Smart showed that Milton's supposed irregularities and innovations, and his departures from what Hallam called 'the best Italian structure', had all been anticipated in Italy, and indicated Della Casa as perhaps the most important of Milton's forerunners in these matters. He

---

[1] With reference to the sonnet on his 'three and twentieth year', in the draft letter contained in the Trinity manuscript.

pointed out that the 'prosody' of Milton's sonnets cannot be understood in isolation:

> As examples of his treatment of verse, the sonnets stand mid-
> way between the simpler style of *Comus*, and that of *Paradise
> Lost*, with its sentences 'variously drawn out from one verse into
> another'. . . . In his epic style he gains both beauty of sound and
> effective emphasis by an unexpected ending at an unusual part
> of the line, metre and meaning being separated or opposed, in-
> stead of being combined with monotonous uniformity.
>
> This is one of the secrets of his later art in blank verse: but it
> was already applied in the sonnets before the epic was begun.[1]

These conclusions remain valid when considered in
the wider context of the present study. Smart relates
Milton's sonnets to Della Casa and to Milton's own
later blank verse; in relating Milton's blank verse to its
Italian analogues one comes back to Della Casa and
his associates. Tasso's *Heroic Sonnets* and his experiments in epic blank verse are links in the chain of
relationships. To give a total picture was beyond the
scope of Smart's investigation of the sonnets; but he
gave a complete picture as far as he went. And after a
wider survey, one finds it is necessary only to adjust
some details of his account, and to change its emphasis
by going somewhat farther into technical analysis.

II

If we accept the probability that Milton's arrangement of his poems was based upon the chronology of
their composition, his sonnets may be divided into two
groups, separated by an interval of about ten years. The
first group, from Sonnet I to Sonnet VII, includes the

---

[1] *The Sonnets of Milton* (Glasgow, 1921), Introduction, pp. 27–28.

poems in Italian; the second begins with the sonnet *When the Assault was intended to the City*, which may be dated 1642, and ends with the sonnet written after the death of his second wife.

In spite of the fact that there are only two sonnets in English in the first group, it is possible to trace within its limits the emergence of Milton's mature conception of the form, and to relate this directly to his Italian studies and exercises. Sonnet I, the Sonnet to the Nightingale, is not only in mood and tone the least Miltonic of the English sonnets; it is also alone in not using those devices of phrasing which are characteristic of all Italian sonnets, and of which Milton shows such a complete grasp in the rest of his sonnets in English. Now Sonnet VII, on his 'three and twentieth year', shows a noticeable number of these very devices. It seems certain that Milton had learnt their use and importance from the experiment of writing the six poems in Italian which his own arrangement places between Sonnet I and Sonnet VII.

In order to make the technical development clear it is necessary to indicate the relation between the sonnet-form and these devices of diction, and to look at Milton's Italian sonnets for evidence of his effort to master them.

III

The sonnet-form has well earned its reputation for encouraging facile artifice. The manufacture of sonnets in Italy has left a great mass of poetry which, though it is on the whole well turned and finished, is of a distressingly mechanical quality. This remorseless exploitation of the sonnet is directly related to the inherent necessities, the unwritten laws, which it imposes on the writer: more than any other form which has survived in modern European literature, it tends to perpetuate fixed methods of expression, and therefore of thought, of feeling.

The necessities and opportunities of the Italian sonnet-form have not always been understood by English poets or by their critics. Since its revival in the Romantic period there has, however, persisted a sense that the sonnet has such unwritten laws, which have sometimes been formulated in a more or less arbitrary manner. It has been said that the 'subject' of a sonnet must make a turn at the eighth line, that the poem must rise like a wave to the eighth line and fall in the sextet, that the second quatrain must develop a statement made in the first, and so on.[1] In fact the effects of the form on the content are at once simpler and more far-reaching, and therefore more difficult to define. The internal divisions and the scheme of rhymes of the Italian sonnet impose a certain parallelism or balance on the whole poem. The movement of quatrains or tercets may be affected or determined by this parallelism; but so are individual words and phrases, and the unfolding of whole sentences and trains of thought.

This parallelism or duplex structure dominates the whole shape of the poem and all its parts, including the smallest phrases. It is not always easy to see it at work, partly because the process may become unconscious and automatic in a practised poet, partly because it is often his purpose to disguise it. The balanced units may be equivalent to each other in subtly irregular ways (in which, of course, the logic of the statement plays a part no less than the language used). The transitions between these units may be so veiled, or disguised by

---

[1] One of J. S. Smart's achievements was to dispose of these arbitrary decrees.

small interpolations, that it is not possible to expound the structure we apprehend. Moreover, the impression of a final unity is always one of the chief aims of a sonnet, and this in itself distracts attention from the manner in which the poem is internally divided and balanced.

An example of the systematic application of parallelism, balance, and antithesis may be seen in the following sonnet by Petrarch, whose work would suffice in itself to show the capacity for concentrated artifice inherent in the form:

> *Sennuccio, i' vo' che sapi in qual manera*
> *Trattato sono e qual vita è la mia:*
> *Ardomi e struggo ancor com' io solia;*
> *L'aura mi volve, e son pur quel ch'i' m'era.*
> *Qui tutta umìle, e qui la vidi altera,*
> *Or aspra or piana, or dispietata or pia;*
> *Or vestirsi onestate, or leggiadria;*
> *Or mansueta, or disdegnosa e fera.*
> *Qui cantò dolcemente, e qui s'assise;*
> *Qui si rivolse, e qui rattenne il passo;*
> *Qui co' begli occhi mi trafisse il core;*
> *Qui disse una parola, e qui sorrise;*
> *Qui cangiò 'l viso. In questi pensier, lasso!*
> *Notte e dì tienmi il signor nostro, Amore.*[1]

Such a lucid symmetry is less often to be seen in the

---

[1] Petrarch, *Il Canzoniere* (Milano, 1925), No. CXII: 'Sennuccio, I wish thee to know in what way I am treated, and what is my life: I burn and destroy myself still as I was wont; the air [*l'aura* = Laura] whirls me about, and yet I am what I was.

'Here I saw her all lowly, and there proud; now harsh, now smooth, now unpitying and now kind; now clothed in majesty, and now in mirth; now gentle, and now disdainful and cruel.

'Here she sang sweetly, and here she seated herself; here she turned back, and here she stayed her step; here with her lovely eyes she pierced my heart;

'Here she uttered a word, and here smiled; here she changed her expression. In these thoughts, alas! night and day I am held by our lord, Love.'

Petrarchan sonneteers of the sixteenth century; they found it more to their taste to enrich and complicate the surface of the sonnet, but they could not, and did not wish to, discard its inner logic. The secret of even the most sophisticated sonnets of Della Casa lies in retaining the old underlying equilibrium beneath a sur-face which is often elaborately irregular.

The structural principle of parallelism in the sonnet may be traced everywhere in the phraseology of Italian examples. In Milton's sonnets in Italian we see him deliberately accepting, studying, and reproducing this type of phraseology. In these poems, as in their models, adjectives and substantives (for example) occur more often than not in pairs; and there is a marked tendency for these pairs to be placed at the end of the lines, so that the second element is emphasized by the rhyme:[1]

> *E' i don' che son d'Amor* saette *ed* arco
> And the gifts which are of Love the arrows and bow
> (Sonnet II)
>
> *Va bagnando l' erbetta* strana *e* bella
> Is wont to wet the strange and lovely plant (Sonnet III)
>
> *Perchè tu scrivi in lingua* ignota *e* strana
> Why dost thou write in tongue unknown and strange
> (Canzone)
>
> *Parte* rinchiusa *e* turbida *si cela*
> Part closed within and turbid hides itself   (Sonnet V)
>
> *Quivi d'attorno o* s'agghiaccia *o* s'ingiela
> Here all round it freezes or congeals   (Sonnet V)

These pairs of adjectives, substantives, and verbs can be expanded into a fuller pattern by entering into

---

[1] The 'rhetoric of rhyme' which dominates the *canzone*, and which affected Milton's use of rhyme in *Lycidas*, is illustrated in a concentrated form in the Italian sonnet.

nation, as they do in the following examples
he same poems:

'erbosa val di Reno e il nobil varco
The grassy vale of the Reno and the famous ford
(Sonnet II)

Quando tu vaga parli, o lieta canti,
Guardi ciascun agli occhi ed agli orecchi
L'entrata[1]
When thou speak'st charmingly, or gaily sing'st,
Let each watch to his eyes and to his ears
The entry   (Sonnet II)

Deh! foss' il mio cuor lento e 'l duro seno
Ah! would my tardy heart and my hard breast
(Sonnet III)

Nè treccie d'oro nè guancia vermiglia
Neither tress of gold nor cheek of red   (Sonnet IV)

Giovane piano, e semplicetto amante
An open youth, and simple-hearted lover (Sonnet VI)

And the balanced phrasing apparent in these single
lines is not, of course, confined within such limits: it
extends to whole sentences and sequences. Sonnet VI,
the last of the series, provides an excellent example of
this; antithesis and balance in individual lines reinforce a similar pattern in the whole statement:

Quando rugge il gran mondo, e scocca il tuono,
S'arma di se, e d'intero diamante,
Tanto del forse, e d'invidia sicuro,
Di timori, e speranze al popol use
Quanto d'ingegno, e d'alto valor vago
E di cetra sonora, e delle muse:

When the great heavens roar and flies the thunder,
(His heart) stands armed in itself and in pure diamond,

[1] The lines recall Della Casa's imitation of the Horatian *dulce ridentem*:
Colà 've dolce parli o dolce rida
Bella donna (Sonetto LIII).

As much secure from envy and from chance,
From fears and hopes such as the many use,
As it is fain of virtue and high thought
And of the sounding lyre and of the Muse.

To look at the Sonnet to the Nightingale and
'three and twentieth year' Sonnet in search of the
Italian mannerisms is to find exactly at what point th
entered Milton's English verse. The Sonnet to th
Nightingale is indeed Italian in its form and manner.
It recalls Bembo in its slightly solemn trifling, its very
literary tone, and even in the epigrammatic turn of its
conclusion. It achieves the total effect of balance and
unity demanded by the form. But in the details of its
diction it shows none of the minutely applied parallelism found in Milton's Italian poems. Now the 'three
and twentieth year' Sonnet has not only a ring of new-
found confidence, as if Milton were surer of his grasp
of the form, but it shows that this confidence must have
come from his Italian exercises. The quatrains are more
carefully distinguished and internally balanced than in
the Sonnet to the Nightingale, and in the tercets the
poem makes its assertions with a striking outburst of
those parallelisms which we have seen Milton practising in Italian:

Yet be it *less* or *more*, or *soon* or *slow*,
  It shall be still in strictest measure eev'n,
  To that same lot, however *mean*, or *high*,
Toward which *Time* leads me, and *the will of Heav'n*;
  All is, if I have grace to use it so,
  As ever in my great task Masters eye.

In the series of his mature sonnets which began about
ten years later with the sonnet *When the Assault was
intended to the City* Milton consistently applies this type
of Italianate phrasing.

combi?e is one further point to be made about this
from t?d of writing verse both in Italian and in English:
I involves a constant tendency towards pleonasm.
only necessary to look back at the examples al/
y given from Milton's Italian or English sonnets
see how parallelism, duplex structure, balanced or
ithetic diction can lead to elegant variation, a pre/
minance of the number of words used over the
number of things said. Neither Milton nor his Italian
exemplars could have been unaware of this inherent ten/
dency to pleonasm, nor of its dangers. It was an accepted
factor in this type of poetry, and the poet's skill was to
be manifested rather in the way in which he could play
with it and disguise it than in any attempt to eliminate it.

The element of pleonasm provides yet another link
between Milton's sonnets and his epic blank verse.
How to achieve a constant, impressive fullness of state/
ment without appearing to inflate the verse was a
problem implicit in the ideal of the 'magnificent' style,
and in no form was it likely to be more difficult to
solve than in blank verse. In Milton's sonnets we see
him exercising a kind of controlled pleonasm, which
he has learnt from Italian example how to develop and
guide and sustain by means of certain metrical and
linguistic tricks. This experience serves him well in his
epic poetry.[1]

IV

The Italian poems as a whole, remarkable as they
are, reveal themselves on consideration as a daring ex/
periment rather than as an achieved poetic success. The
precise date of their composition may remain uncertain,
but it would be before Milton's twenty/fourth birthday,
if the connexion between their diction and that of

[1] See p. 123.

Sonnet VII is accepted. They would then belong to a period of Milton's life when he had expressed personal sentiments as yet only in Latin: they may confirm that he instinctively preferred the protection of an alien tongue and a literary convention when it was a matter of seeing himself as a young lover.

The language and convention of Bembo, his special development of the Petrarchan manner, enabled Milton to represent himself as a poet, a scholar, and a reluctant lover. The poems in Italian are less love-poems than slightly amorous compliments. Milton could scarcely lose self-consciousness in a passion so largely literary in nature. The greater part of the little group of poems is concerned with the oddity of his writing poetry in a foreign language: this oddity is explained by the further oddity of his finding himself in love. Sonnets II and V, which are more purely love-poems, are unconvincing. Indeed the latter, in attempting a description of Milton's intimate emotions, is the most frigid of all.

Milton's difficulties in expressing his own tempera-ment in the conventions of Petrarchan love-poetry are suggested by the conclusion of Sonnet III. The gist of the poem is that he cultivates the flower of an alien tongue as a 'shepherdess' would carefully foster an exotic plant in an uncongenial climate: why does he thus exchange the fair Thames for the fair Arno?

> *Amor lo volse, ed io a l'altrui peso*
> *Seppi ch' Amor cosa mai volse indarno.*
> *Deh! foss' il mio cuor lento e 'l duro seno*
> *A chi pianta dal ciel si buon terreno.*[1]

The conflict between human love and the love of God has been mentioned as one of the fundamental themes

---

[1] 'Love wished it so, and I from the burden of others knew that Love never wished anything in vain. Ah! would that my tardy heart and my hard bosom were as good a soil to him who plants from Heaven.'

in Petrarchan verse.[1] But Milton, in adopting it from his models, has surely failed to convince us that it faith-fully reflects his own experience. It may well be that, during the years of his conscious pupilage to which these poems seem to belong, he was reluctant to be distracted from his studies by seriously falling in love. But the note of reluctant worldliness, the 'penitential' view of love which the Petrarchan tradition implies, is alien to Milton's moral temper. He expresses himself far more effectively in the conscious nobility, the bold self-righteousness, of Sonnet VI, which in sentiment is by far the most individual of the series:

> Giovane piano, e semplicetto amante
>> Poi che fuggir me stesso in dubbio sono
>> Madonna a voi del mio cuor l'umil dono
>> Farò divoto; io certo a prove tante
> L'hebbi fedele, intrepido, costante,
>> De pensieri leggiadro, accorto, e buono;
>> Quando rugge il gran mondo, e scocca il tuono
>> S'arma di se, e d'intero diamante,
> Tanto del forse, e d'invidia sicuro,
>> Di timori, e speranze al popol use
>> Quanto d'ingegno, e d'alto valor vago,
> E di cetra sonora, e delle muse:
>> Sol troverete in tal parte men duro
>> Ove amor mise l'insanabil ago.[2]

---

[1] See p. 25.

[2] 'An open youth and a simple lover, since I am doubtful whether I can flee myself, Madonna, I will devote to you the humble gift of my heart; certain it is I have kept it through many trials faithful, intrepid and unwavering, in its thoughts happy, well-disciplined and kind; when the vast heavens roar and the thunder flies, it arms itself in itself and in entire diamond, as much secure from envy and from chance, from fears and hopes such as the many use, as it is fain of thought and of high virtue, and of the sounding lyre and of the Muses: only you will find it less hard in that part where Love has fixed his cureless sting.'

This self-portrait is of the true Miltonic temper, and anticipates the 'self-esteem, grounded on just and right' of many of the English sonnets.

It is difficult for English critics to speak with confidence of the linguistic and technical qualities of Milton's Italian poems. Certainly, whatever their deficiencies, they testify to an astonishing literary genius. And Milton's command of Italian surely shows, despite any imperfections of idiom,[1] an altogether personal feeling for the language—a capacity for responding to its special movement and music. It may be said, however, that in these Italian sonnets he had chosen for his models writers whose style allowed for a certain difficulty of utterance. Professor Praz has qualified these poems as *bembista*; it may be pointed out also that Milton at this date already knew the poetry of Della Casa,[2] and that the example of both these poets might have led him to think that the undoubted difficulty and even harshness of his own verse in Italian was wholly permissible. He might have been far less ready to try his hand at poems in Italian if his only model had been Petrarch, renowned for smooth perfection, lucidity, and symmetry of construction. Bembo's Latinate intricacy of syntax, and Della Casa's further loosening of the rhythmic pattern of the sonnet—though these things were a product of the highest art—rendered their manner less resistant to imitation by a foreigner, or at least by a foreigner with Milton's special poetic gifts.

The example of Bembo and Della Casa was probably taken by Milton to justify what is found every-

[1] Carducci praises Milton's enterprise, but adds: '. . . i più son duri e stentati e talora in onta alle leggi più strette della sintassi.' *Opere* (Bologna, 1921), ii. 458.

[2] Professor Praz mentions Milton's Italian poems in his *Rapporti tra la letteratura italiana e la letteratura inglese*, p. 168. Milton wrote his name in his copy of Della Casa's *Prose et Poesie* in 1629.

where in these sonnets, the disregard for the divisions between quatrains and tercets. In the degree to which it is carried by Milton this is not characteristic even of Della Casa, whose work was strongly marked by it, but who always preserves a sense of the familiar under-lying patterns. No doubt Milton's irregularities in this respect are due mainly to the inevitable limits of his control of the language, for in his English sonnets he captures instead the delicate balance required: the stanza-form survives the modulations in his English as it does not in his Italian. However, his transgressions may also have been due, at this early stage of his Italian studies, to some degree of misunderstanding on his part. That his technical insight was not yet complete may be gathered from his calling a *canzone* a poem which, however accomplished in achieving its desired effect, is not a *canzone*. From the point of view of mastery of the medium this is indeed the most successful of his Italian poems:

> *Ridonsi donne e giovani amorosi*
> *M'accostandosi attorno, e perche scrivi,*
> *Perche tu scrivi in lingua ignota e strana*
> *Verseggiando d'amor, e come t'osi?*
> *Dinne, se la tua speme sia mai vana,*
> *E de pensieri lo miglior t'arrivi;*
> *Cosi mi van burlando, altri rivi*
> *Altri lidi t'aspettan, & altre onde*
> *Nelle cui verdi sponde*
> *Spuntati ad hor, ad hor a la tua chioma*
> *L'immortal guiderdon d'eterne frondi*
> *Perche alle spalle tue soverchia soma?*
> > *Canzon dirotti, e tu per me rispondi*
> > *Dice mia Donna, e 'l suo dir, è il mio cuore*
> > *Questa è lingua di cui si vanta Amore.*[1]

[1] 'Ladies and young men in love laugh, clustering about me, and "Why dost write, why dost thou write in an unknown and alien

The poem is not without its flaws, among which must be reckoned touches of obscurity and elliptical syntax. But in its freer grace of movement it serves to demonstrate once more that Milton was happier in such an improvised pattern of rhymes than he could be in the more confined space of the sonnet-form. It is true that in the Italian sonnets he allows himself to transgress the stanzaic character of the form; but that is precisely the fault of the poems, that he does so too freely, owing to the handicap of the language. The full measure of his powers could only appear in poetry in his own tongue. Consequently Milton's most worthy and impressive following of his sixteenth-century Italian models is to be found in his English sonnets, where he shows that he appreciates both the limits and the opportunities of the 'heroic' form.

V

Milton's Sonnet on his 'three and twentieth year', taken in conjunction with the Italian poems and the Sonnet to the Nightingale, indicates that it was with his conception of 'the Petrarchian stanza' as it was with his conceptions of epic and tragedy. He acquires in his youth a conception of these literary forms as they were approved or practised by the Italians of the later Renaissance. His middle age and his old age see him

tongue, versifying of love, and how dost dare? Tell us, so may thy hope be not in vain, and may a better thought come to thee." So they proceed to mock me, "Other shores, other coasts are waiting for thee, and other waves on whose green banks budded even now for thy locks the immortal prize of eternal leaves. Why [take] upon thy shoulders this superfluous burden?"
' My song, I shall say to thee, and thou answer for me, " My Lady says, and her word is my heart's will, *This is the language of which Love makes boast*".'

carrying out in his poetry critical principles and conceptions of form settled once for all ten, twenty, or thirty years earlier.

So the series of English sonnets written between about 1642 and 1658 can scarcely be called poetic experiments, though with them a new technical interest enters into Milton's verse. They are not experiments, they are not even perhaps exercises, if these expressions suggest some uncertainty in the poet's control of his medium. But the complexity of the wordorder and the development of the rhythm in these poems for the first time approach the diction and rhythm of the epics; and it seems clear that for Milton these occasional poems were closely related to the conception of style which he was holding in reserve for his great work.

The sonnets are therefore essays, on a small scale, in the 'magnificent' style; and Milton confines his topics to such as could appropriately be presented in this stately garb. Certainly, if the majority of his sonnets are on religious or political themes, the proper field of heroic verse, a few may be distinguished as verging upon the mockheroic: the more intimate, and particularly the convivial invitations to his young pupils, have the Horatian quality of something approaching selfparody. The controversial sonnets also turn the stiff difficulty of the verse, the *asprezza* of the 'magnificent' style, to a mocking purpose.

All this is sufficiently personal, and indeed the force of Milton's sonnets consists essentially in their springing (like *Lycidas*) out of immediate and intense circumstances. Yet enough has been said of the Renaissance tradition which they follow to make it clear how closely they adhere to that formal heritage. Milton thinks only of himself and of his subject; but his poetry follows

Della Casa, in so far as it is based upon a complete identity of principles. It is scarcely worth the trouble to single out small tricks of style, detailed verbal resemblances, or resemblances of movement, when these affinities are due to the deeper kinship of mood and manner.

The plotting of this general relationship between Milton and his Italian models has indeed been done very effectively by J. S. Smart. There is but one important feature of the English sonnets which deserves more emphasis than Smart gives, and that is the complexity of the wordorder: not only for its own predominant function in the beauty of the poems, but for its derivation from the Italian tradition. It is the artificiality of the wordorder which makes possible the special beauties of both Della Casa and Milton. This alone makes possible the continuous interplay of the expected and the unexpected, the transformation of occasional verse into singular and vivid poetry. Just as in any prose translation or transcription of a sonnet by Della Casa the charm of the poem evaporates in a series of flat or pompous statements, so if we 'normalize' the wordorder in a sonnet by Milton (or suspend our response to the music and movement of the language) there seems little left to admire.[1]

Yet the underlying prosequality often to be detected in the sonnets is as much a source of strength as of weakness; it is just the way in which this rational plainness, this solidity, become poetic, that

[1] Italian critics were fond of observing, with Sertorio Quattromani, how often Della Casa *sovra un concetto vulgare forma un sonetto divino*: 'From which one can see', adds Quattromani, 'that it is not the thoughts which make a Poet, as some would have us believe, but the locutions . . .' (quoted in Della Casa, *Opere*, v. 48).

may excite most admiration. Take as an example
Sonnet IX:

> Lady that in the prime of earliest youth,
>> Wisely hath shun'd the broad way and the green,
>> And with those few art eminently seen,
>> That labour up the Hill of heav'nly Truth,
> The better part with *Mary* and with *Ruth*,
>> Chosen thou hast, and they that overween,
>> And at thy growing vertues fret their spleen,
>> No anger find in thee, but pity and ruth.
> Thy care is fixt and zealously attends
>> To fill thy odorous Lamp with deeds of light,
>> And Hope that reaps not shame. Therefore be sure
> Thou, when the Bridegroom with his feastfull friends
>> Passes to bliss at the mid hour of night,
>> Hast gain'd thy entrance, Virgin wise and pure.

The poem contains no thought which could be considered ingenious or profound or, in its context, unusual. The special quality of the statements made is
rather that they are appropriate, and recognizably so at
a first rehearsal. In this respect it shows, like Della
Casa's compliments, the value, for serious poetry, of
the critical idea of decorum. As for the poetic 'realization' of the thoughts: the images of which the poet
avails himself are all more or less allegorical in nature,
and remain so, for all the freshness or force he imparts
to them. We have thus 'the broad way and the green'
deriving from the New Testament; 'the Hill of heav'nly
Truth', a moral and poetic commonplace; the 'lamp'
and the 'Bridegroom' come, of course, from the parable
of the Wise and the Foolish Virgins, and retain their
simple picturesque beauty, heightened by the mildly
rich language and metaphor: 'odorous', 'deeds of light',
'Hope that reaps not shame', 'feastful friends', and 'the
mid hour of night'.

The beauty of the poem resides only partially in these elements of image and metaphor, which are all spiritualized and allegorical. It is to be found far more in the sound of the words, in relation to the movement of the thought. Both thought and words are carefully arranged, or disarranged. Incomplete phrases and clauses are inverted and interpolated, then completed, in a way absolutely new in English poetry, and which heightens the reader's attention and brings out the value of every syllable. There is thus an impression of rigour and tension, even when the thought is not in itself difficult. Milton emphasizes equally the end of his lines and the end of his sentences, both when they coincide and when they part company; thus he takes advantage both of the rigid complex rhyme-scheme and of the freedom of his periods, and gains an effect of weight by increasing the number of strong pauses he can make in what remains a short poem. In his choice of rhymes and other words he is influenced by the *asprezza* of his Italian models: that is, he likes strong and contrasting and slightly unusual sounds. The parallelistic phrasing which comes from the Italian sonnets is very evident and carefully placed in relation to the line-endings.

Sonnet IX is an example of deliberately exquisite writing in the Italian manner. But Milton's sonnets do not always give an impression of such calm, transparent, restraint. The sonnet *On the late Massacher in Piemont* and the first sonnet on his blindness show that his tendency, when more deeply moved, was to handle the form with very great boldness. In the pauses multiplied within their lines, and the abruptness and bareness of certain of their sentences, these sonnets carry Della Casa's innovations much farther than any poet had ever done in Italian.

The total impression left by Milton's mere handful of sonnets is of a more salient genius than that of any sonnet writer in sixteenth-century Italy. Many external factors no doubt contributed to the greater intensity of Milton's verse within these narrow limits. England's national temper was raised to a high pitch of enthusiasm in those years of the seventeenth century, and if the religious and political conflict was deep and bitter, it had its tragic and heroic compensations. Milton's personal situation and experience were no less remarkable, and he was fully qualified to give them voice in these poems.

A comparison between the general poetic achievement of these English sonnets and that of their Italian exemplars therefore reveals the same kind and degree of difference that we find in a comparison between Milton's blank verse and that of Tasso.[1] The English poet has the advantage, which is not to be underestimated, of doing something new in his time and country. This is a part of the greater freshness and vigour of his particular tradition at that particular time, as compared with the artistic tradition to which he looks back. The inherent capacities of the two languages come out also as factors in this type of verse. English is incapable of much that Italian can do; but an element of plainness and harshness which it can bring to the 'magnificent' style gives it a certain advantage in this field.

[1] See p. 120.

7

MILTON'S BLANK VERSE:
THE DICTION

I

THERE is a decisive change of tone in Milton's verse after 1638, a sudden access of confidence, which one may well attribute to his Italian travels; and this suggests that those travels themselves may have been undertaken with a precise literary purpose which had found what it sought. It seems possible that Milton's studies had led him to a point, in 1638, at which he found he must seek information in Italy itself concerning the methods and theories of heroic poetry. He went first to Florence for the tradition of critical analysis and discussion; he sought out Manso in Rome and Naples because he wished to find out all he could about Tasso, the only epic poet of modern times of whom he thoroughly approved.

However, even if we can never be sure that the tradition of epic 'magnificence' in Italian was a prime object of Milton's journey, we can assert that, as a result of his experience in Italy, he found it. The evidence of the texts is clear. At some time in these three or four years Milton had seized the idea of the 'magnificent' style in Italian, and decided to adopt its methods in English. His abnormal literary faculty made this seem a comparatively simple matter. There are no signs of

faltering in the sonnets; and there is no reason to sup/
pose that, if *Paradise Lost* had been written in the 1640's,
it would have been stylistically less perfect than it is.

It becomes less difficult to account for the technical
skill of *Paradise Lost* if we place it against the back/
ground of Italian Renaissance verse. Just as Milton
had several perfectly accomplished Italian models for
his type of sonnet, he had an Italian tradition of epic
blank verse with which to reinforce the style and dic/
tion of *Paradise Lost*. It is true that in Italy no un/
deniably great work had yet been written in this form;
the metre was not to attain its full glory there until the
eighteenth century, when Parini surpassed all other
didactic poets in infusing Virgilian grandeur into
the descriptive satire of *Il Giorno*. But this eighteenth/
century achievement, and the admirable blank verse
of the Romantic period which followed it, had itself
been prepared for by the experiments of the *Cinque/
cento*: Milton in England did but develop the Italian
epic tradition as it might well have been developed in
Italy itself in the seventeenth century, had it not been
for the failure of creative power which then came to
Italian literature.

Blank verse in Italian was the invention of the
Cinquecento.[1] Yet the attempts to perfect it as an
instrument for epic poetry were for one reason or
another unsuccessful. Trissino's *Italia Liberata* failed
from sheer poverty of poetic energy and imagination.
Caro's translation of the *Aeneid* was a most remarkable
performance, but, far from raising his *versi sciolti* to the

[1] Carducci refers to a thirteenth-century blank-verse poem by
Brunetto Latini and to a fourteenth-century Venetian author's use
of blank verse for a series of love-epistles in the manner of Ovid;
but he makes it clear that the metre only developed fully with the
spread of classical studies in the sixteenth century ('Il Parini Maggiore',
Storia del 'Giorno', *Opere* (Bologna, 1933), xiv. 279–82).

grave beauty of Virgil's hexameters, Caro rather brought the Roman epic down to the familiarity, ease, and delightful vividness of Tuscan speech.[1] Tasso's *Mondo Creato* was the most ambitious and sustained effort to raise blank verse to the heroic pitch; but it suffered, not only from Tasso's intellectual weaknesses and the weariness of his last years, but from the fact that its matter was not that of the epic proper.[2]

Enough had been done, however, in sixteenth-century Italy, to show the possibilities for epic poetry held out by the new metre. And, moreover, enough had been written by Italian critics to show that they perceived both the dangers and the demands of this form of verse. It was realized that both diction and content must become of special importance when the metre itself imposes so little restraint on the poet. Even before Caro translated the *Aeneid*, the acuteness of a Florentine scholar, Carlo Lenzoni, had defined the problems of blank verse and pointed to its suitability for epic grandeur.

Since one cannot cover up this verse [he wrote] with the sweetness of rhymes, or excuse oneself by the necessity of closing one's sentences, as in *terzetti* and *stanze*; and because, having been released from these demands, it can no longer make use of licences which are in themselves permissible: it does not allow of incorrectness, either in the language or the composition, it does not submit to harshness in the expression nor to weakness in the rhythm, it does not buoy up weak or empty ideas; and in fine it is not enough for it only to do what is necessary, it must also reject anything which is not great in itself or which art cannot make great by virtue of ornamentation and beauty.[3]

[1] See Carducci, op. cit., p. 265.
[2] See Appendix A for specimens of Italian blank verse of the sixteenth century.
[3] *In difesa della lingua fiorentina e di Dante* (Florence, 1556): quoted by Carducci, op. cit., p. 281.

Lenzoni thus anticipated by two centuries Johnson's dictum that 'blank verse, if it be not tumid and gorgeous, is but crippled prose'. The Florentine critic proceeded to argue that these inherent necessities of blank verse must impel it to the expression of heroic grandeur, both in the conception and the language:

Therefore, as being most capable of all gravity and grandeur, and, if one may put it so, most desirous of appearing marvellous to the hearer; and differing from other forms of verse as the eloquent man is said to differ from the pedant: it seeks that point and perfection of excellence contained in the idea of perfect heroic poetry. The marvellous beauty of which kind of poetry (though it can be better apprehended by the mind than by the ear) we have truly no kind of verse which can show us better or more fully than this, coloured not, so to speak, with artificial enamel, but with its own natural blood.[1]

From such criticisms as these, and from the various Italian endeavours to devise an epic form of blank verse, Milton could clearly perceive the vital connexion here between verse and style, measure and manner. If blank verse were to succeed, it must be largely by virtue of some special power or beauty of diction. This was the lesson to be learnt from the *versi sciolti* of the sixteenth century, and it included the recommendation of Virgil as the all-sufficient model for the supreme diction required.

It is in the light of these decisions and discriminations that we must interpret Milton's own statement of the structural principle of his verse: 'the sense variously drawn out from one verse into another'. The structural power of this principle could be developed fully only in blank verse, for only in blank verse could its elaborate application be justified. The basis of both English and Italian prosody was rhyme. Blank verse,

[1] Ibid.: Carducci, op. cit., p. 282.

having discarded this, needed to find some other means of enforcing a continuity of pattern, inducing a con‑ tinuity of expectation in the reader: hence the play of diction and prosody in forms which produce slowness and suspense. The Italians worked out this style with the guidance of such general conceptions as *asprezza*, 'difficulty', and 'magnificence'. Milton accepted their premisses and conclusions, and adopted what he could of their working methods.

II

It is scarcely possible to give more than a token of the relationship between the rich Virgilian texture of *Paradise Lost* and Italian experiments in epic diction. This may be done, however, by taking as an example a verbal pattern which comes down to the sixteenth century from earlier Italian poetry, and is then turned, with elaborations and variations, to the new purposes; and which Milton also makes a part of his epic diction.

A common usage in Italian poetry from Dante and Petrarch onwards is the addition of a second adjective, as an interjection or afterthought, to an already quali‑ fied substantive. This little device was found very useful by Bembo and his followers, and Della Casa employs it frequently as a part of his equipment for suspending the sense and slowing down the movement of his verse:

Or *viver orbo i* gravi *giorni* e rei
Now live bereaved my heavy days and cruel

(Sonetto XIII)

Dolce rigor; cortese *orgoglio* e pio
Sweet severity, courteous disdain and kind (Sonetto XI)

Bella *fera* e gentil *mi punse il seno*
A fair wild beast, and sweet, had pierced my breast

(Sonetto XII)

Fo mesti i boschi, e pii del mio cordoglio
Make sad the woods, and pitiful of my plight

(Sonetto XLI)

In chiaro foco e memorabil arse
In a clear flame and memorable burned

(Sonetto XXXV)

This trick of phrasing is very common in the sonnet form, where there is a constant tendency to arrange words in pairs.[1] Milton introduces it into his English sonnets, and it appears early in *Paradise Lost*:

Before all Temples th'upright heart and pure

(*P.L.*, Book I, l. 18)

In this, its simplest form, it is indeed one of the marks of Milton's diction, and its appearance in any later writer is enough to stamp the verse as 'Miltonic':

High matter thou injoinst me, O prime of men,
Sad task and hard   (*P.L.*, Book V, ll. 563-4)

He comes, and settl'd in his face I see
Sad resolution and secure   (*P.L.*, Book VI, ll. 540-1)

An easy variation is to separate the second adjective, or adjectival phrase, more widely from the first:

Feroce spirto un tempo ebbi e guerrero
A fierce soul once I had, and warlike too

(Della Casa, Sonetto XLVIII)

Aspro costume in bella Donna e rio
Harsh custom in fair lady, and unkind

(Ibid., Sonetto III)

E di sì mansueta e gentil pria,
Barbara fatta sovr' ogn' altra, e fera
And from so mild and well-conditioned once,
Barbarous made above all others, and wild

(Ibid., Sonetto LXI)

[1] See p. 94.

Così deluso il cor più volte, e punto
Dall' aspro orgoglio, piagne
Thus undeceived the heart again, and pierced
By sharp disdain, will weep   (Della Casa, Sonetto V)

                pleasing was his shape,
And lovely   (*P.L.*, Book IX, ll. 503-4)

                for wide was spred
That Warr and various   (*P.L.*, Book VI, ll. 241-2)

For many are the Trees of God that grow
In Paradise, and various, yet unknown
To us   (*P.L.*, Book IX, ll. 618-20)

Faithful hath been your Warfare, and of God
Accepted, fearless in his righteous Cause
                        (*P.L.*, Book VI, ll. 803-4)

It will be seen that these patterns grow in complexity, since the adjectives or participles placed in this way may have attached to them qualifying words or phrases, and these in their turn may be disposed in a similar pattern:

Ben mi scorgea quel dì crudele stella
E di dolor ministra e di martiri
Troth I discerned that day a cruel star,
And of sorrow ministrant and of pains
                        (Della Casa, Sonetto XL)

Ed or di lui si scosse in tutto, e scinse
Tua candida Alma, e leve fatta appieno,
Salìo, son certo, ov' è più il Ciel sereno
And now from (earth) shook wholly free, and purged
Itself, thy white soul, and made light in all,
Climbed up, I know, where most the heavens are pure
                        (Ibid., Sonetto XLV)

the Tree of Life,
The middle Tree and highest there that grew
(P.L., Book IV, ll. 194-5)

others on the grass
Coucht, and, now fild with pasture gazing sat,
Or Bedward ruminating   (P.L., Book IV, ll. 350-2)

then whom a Spirit more lewd
Fell not from Heaven, or more gross to love
Vice for it self   (P.L., Book I, ll. 490-2)

But the full possibilities of such patterns as these only appear when one looks for them without regard for the precise grammatical nature of their components. Substantives or verbs can be placed in this way as easily as adjectives; and the style of *Paradise Lost* is in reality less 'adjectival' than its fullness of statement would suggest. Milton more frequently uses substantives than adjectives in the pattern in question:

Amaze,
Be sure, and terrour seis'd the rebel Host
(P.L., Book VI, ll. 646-7)

when the Scourge
Inexorably, and the torturing houre
(P.L., Book II, ll. 90-91)

he seemd
For dignity compos'd and high exploit
(P.L., Book II, ll. 110-11)

Italian examples are not far to seek:

Ov' è 'l silenzio, che 'l dì fugge, e 'l lume?
Where is silence, that the day flees, and the light?
(Della Casa, Sonetto L)

Già fu valore, e chiaro sangue accolto
Inseme, e cortesia
One time were valour and noble blood received
Together, and courtesy   (Della Casa, Sonetto LIV)

                e ghiaccio
Gli spiriti anch' io sento, e le membra farsi
                and ice
My spirits too I feel, and limbs, become
                    (Ibid., Sonetto LVIII)

Even more constant and varied use is made of substantives combined with adjectives in this way, because
the placing of the adjectives before or after their nouns
can be made to contribute to the deliberate complex
balance:

Mansueto odio spero, e pregion pia
Mild hatred I may hope, and prison kind
                    (Ibid., Sonetto XXVII)

Mai io palustre augel, che poco s'erga
Sull 'ale, sembro, o luce inferma, e lume
Ch'a leve aura vacille, e si consume
But I some marshland bird, that scarce can rise
On pinions, seem, or some faint light or lamp
That to a slight breath wavers, and is spent
                    (Ibid., Sonetto XLIX)

Che più crudo Euro a me mio verno adduce,
Più lunga notte, e dì più freddi e scarsi
For harsher winds to me my winter brings,
A longer night, and days more chilled and drear
                    (Ibid., Sonetto LVIII)

So pray'd they innocent, and to thir thoughts
Firm peace recoverd soon and wonted calm
                    (*P.L.*, Book V, ll. 209–10)

                his gestures fierce
He markd and mad demeanour, then alone
                    (*P.L.*, Book IV, ll. 128–9)

> for his sleep
> Was Aerie light, from pure digestion bred,
> And temperat vapors bland, which th' only sound
> Of leaves and fuming rills, Aurora's fan,
> Lightly dispers'd, and the shrill Matin Song
> Of Birds on every bough   (*P.L.*, Book V, ll. 3–8)

The last example illustrates beautifully how such patterns enrich themselves as they unfold, by a sort of
natural impetus which they gather; that is to say, once
the pattern imposes itself and its movement, numerous
floating phrases may be attached to the central statement. Adjectives may be balanced against adverbial
phrases or participles:

> From Diamond Quarries hew'n & Rocks of Gold
> (*P.L.*, Book V, l. 756)

> but torture without end
> Still urges, and a fiery Deluge, fed
> With ever-burning Sulphur unconsum'd
> (*P.L.*, Book I, ll. 67–69)

> From thence a Rib, with cordial spirits warme,
> And Life-blood streaming fresh
> (*P.L.*, Book VIII, ll. 467–8)

The following passages show the same movement in
various degrees of complexity and force:

> *Nè quale ingegno è 'n voi colto, e ferace,*
> *Cosmo, nè scorto in nobil arte il vero*
> *Nè retto con virtù tranquillo impero,*
> *Nè loda, nè valor sommo e verace*
> Neither what mind is in you skilled and keen,
> Cosmo, nor spied by noble science truth,
> Nor steered with rectitude a peaceful realm,
> Nor fame, nor worth exalted and most pure
> (Della Casa, Sonetto XXII)

Perocch' a noi, com' alla fertil vite,
Conviensi, o come alla feconda oliva,
Producer largamente i dolci frutti

Because to us, as to the fertile vine,
Becoming 'tis, or to the fecund olive,
To bring forth in abundance our sweet fruits

> (Tasso, *Mondo Creato*, Giornata Terza)

      but nigh at Hand
Celestial Armourie, Shields, Helmes, and Speares,
Hung high, with Diamond flaming and with Gold

> (*P.L.*, Book IV, ll. 552-4)

      as with Starrs thir bodies all
And Wings were set with Eyes, with Eyes the Wheels
Of Beril, and careering Fires between

> (*P.L.*, Book VI, ll. 754-6).

A comparison between Tasso's and Milton's skill in such writing might be drawn from the following passages, two of them on the whole pedestrian, and two eloquent:

E nell' istesso modo
Fa ritrosa la Luna, e 'l suo bel cerchio
Finge ineguale, e non ritondo appieno,
E la figura le distorce, e 'l corso

      And in the self-same manner
Makes err the Moon, and her fair circle feigns
Uneven, and not rounded to the full,
And both her face distorts, and wayward course

> (Tasso, *Mondo Creato*, Giornata Quarta)

      the floating Vessel swum
Uplifted; and secure with beaked prow
Rode tilting o're the Waves, all dwellings else
Flood overwhelmd, and with them all thir pomp
Deep under water rould; Sea cover'd Sea,
Sea without shoar; and in thir Palaces,

Where luxurie late reign'd, Sea-monsters whelp'd
And stabl'd; of Mankind, so numerous late,
All left, in one small bottom swum imbark't.

(P.L., Book XI, ll. 741–9)

Oh! piaccia a lui, che ne distringe, e lega,
Com' a lui piace, e talor solve, e snoda
I lacci del peccato, e i duri nodi,
Onde 'l fato quaggiù tien l'alme avvinte
Oh! may it please Him who distrains and binds,
As pleases Him, and sometimes melts and solves
The thongs of sin, and those hard knots wherein
Fate here below detains our captive souls

(Tasso, Mondo Creato, Giornata Seconda)

Standing on Earth, not rapt above the Pole,
More safe I Sing with mortal voice, unchang'd
To hoarse or mute, though fall'n on evil dayes,
On evil dayes though fall'n, and evil tongues;
In darkness, and with dangers compast round,
And solitude;   (<i>P.L.</i>, Book VII, ll. 23–28)

Even within the narrow limits of these quotations it may be seen that the conception of style and the methods of the two poets are identical; and also that there is a greater force and vividness of expression, and freshness of feeling, in Milton than in Tasso.

III

A close comparison between Milton's diction and that of these sixteenth-century Italians suggests that, while English is less capable than Italian of imitating certain details of Latin syntax, our language is, on the other hand, a more flexible instrument and can there-fore sustain this rich Virgilian manner with greater

ease and variety. Thus we find that the texture of
Milton's epic diction is more uniformly fine than that
of Tasso's *Mondo Creato*, in which a certain monotony
and flatness makes itself felt, and appears clearly in the
repetition of phrases such as *i stellanti chiostri* for the sky.
The richness and delicacy of Milton's language can
bear comparison even with the concentrated beauty of
Della Casa's sonnets, in spite of the difference in scale
and perspective between epic narrative and a lyric of
fourteen lines.

The explanation is probably to be found in part in
the relative freedom of English from syntactical bonds.
This may be shown even within the limits of the little
verbal pattern whose varied possibilities have just been
illustrated. While Milton can, for example, use his
adjectives very frequently with an adverbial effect, the
Italian poets are more restricted to the primary grammatical function of their words. *Paradise Lost* is full of
such adverbial adjectives as in this passage:

>   for wide was spred
> That Warr and various   (*P.L.*, Book VI, ll. 241-2)

And this use of adjectives is, of course, prevalent as a
vulgar solecism in spoken English. In Milton's Italian
models such constructions are indeed to be found:

>   *chi vede Marte*
> *Gli altrui campi inondar torbido insano*
>   he who sees Mars
> Another's fields inundate turbid and foul
>   (Della Casa, Sonetto XLVI)

> *Nel sacro monte, ov' oggi uom rado viene*
> On the holy hill where now men rarely come
>   (Ibid., Sonetto XXV)

> *Ov' orma di virtù raro s'imprime*
> Where print of virtue's foot is rarely pressed
>   (Ibid., Sonetto XXVI)

And participles in Italian can quite easily be used with this effect:

> *Ahi venen nova, che piacendo ancide!*
> Ah novel poison, that by pleasing kills!
>
> (Ibid., Sonetto LIII)

> *Mira, Padre celeste, omai con quante*
> *Lacrime a Te devoto mi converto*
> See, Heavenly Father, henceforth with how many
> Tears unto Thee devout I do me turn
>
> (Ibid., Sonetto LXVI)

But in Italian the demands of syntax make success in this type of diction more strenuous than in English. Parini's *Il Giorno* is the longest poem in which complexity and richness are sustained from beginning to end; and it is on the scale of the *Georgics* rather than, like *Paradise Lost*, on that of the *Aeneid*.

IV

In the pattern of which various forms have been chosen as examples there is only one constant element, and this would be found in any similar pattern that could be chosen and traced: that is, that the sense of the statement is suspended or interrupted. A quite direct, simple, or 'logical' order of words is avoided in order to provide one in which the completion of the statement is either postponed or anticipated.

In some cases it may even be impossible to say what a 'logical' word-order would be. In the lines,

> his gestures fierce
> He mark'd and mad demeanour, then alone,

one might choose to say that 'He marked his gestures fierce and mad demeanour, then alone' would be more logical. But rhetoric, which seeks to reproduce the vividness of impressions, or to give the emphasis of passion, is entirely justified in placing the 'gestures' first. And while it might then seem more logical to say 'His gestures fierce and mad demeanour, then alone, he marked', this would also bring about a loss of vividness and emphasis: the expression would decline into flatness and heaviness.

It is clear, then, that the systematic deformation of 'logical' word-order, as it is applied in Milton, is made to serve the poetic effect both in a narrowly technical and in a more general aesthetic manner. By means of the phrasing the sense is suspended and diffused throughout a larger block of words than could otherwise be built into a unity; verses and sentences are thus bound together and brought into animated movement. Moreover, this intricate word-order is also a conventional method of gaining the effect of emphatic, excited, or passionate modes of speech. This is the language of sublimated emotion and intellectual excitement.[1]

V

Miltonic diction is thus but one aspect of a form of poetry in which everything is unified: matter, meaning, emotion, method. What might appear superficially a mere complexity of ornament, in fact contributes essentially to the structure of the verse, and corresponds to the strength of the 'inspiration', the poetic emotion. The dangers of the style and the diction are obvious enough: the elaboration of language, the complexity of surface, are only justified if the poem requires a fullness of statement which often amounts to pleonasm.

[1] See Coleridge, *Biographia Literaria*, chapters xvi–xviii.

The element of pleonasm is one of the foundations of *Paradise Lost*.[1] And, if the dangers of this pleonastic style are obvious, it is equally obvious that throughout the whole immense length of his poem Milton has succeeded in avoiding the worst of these dangers: inflation, the presenting too little matter and meaning in too many words.

His success can be understood in general terms only as a result of extreme intellectual energy, joined with force of character. But there are minor manifestations of this mental energy which deserve recognition, if only because they have received too little attention in the past. These include his addiction to verbal wit, various forms of conceits, and puns. This is not only more characteristic than has always been admitted, but provides also a parallel to certain features of Tasso's style. Milton has his own particular form of *seicentismo*, and this form is anticipated here and there in Tasso, most obviously in the *Mondo Creato*.

In Milton's epic poetry there is an incessant, sometimes obtrusive, activity of mind at the level of verbal wit: there is play upon words, sometimes in puns, sometimes in emphasizing the jingling qualities of words of different or kindred meaning, sometimes in twisting grotesquely ingenious complexities of syntax. These freaks of fancy are combined with a remorseless chopping of logic, above all in the speeches, which has a similar effect. That effect is above all to compensate for the somewhat stupefying power of the 'magnificent' diction, to add possibilities of surprise to a technique of which one of the chief dangers is monotony. The play upon words and the metaphysical or logical conceits are not indeed alien to this epic style, for

[1] The importance of pleonasm in the sonnets has been already suggested, p. 97.

ingenuity is here omnipresent in one form or another: it is present in the artificial word-order and in the music of the verse no less than in the assiduous search for what is astounding in thought and image and emotion. The whole elaborate machine could only be con-structed and kept moving by a constant exercise of the mind, and it is only by way of variety, and not by any abandonment of principle, that this mental activity sometimes displays itself in such sports as the following:

> Serpent, we might have spar'd our coming hither,
> Fruitless to me, though Fruit be here to excess
> <div align="right">(<i>P.L.</i>, Book IX, ll. 647–8)</div>

> At one slight bound high overleap'd all bound
> Of Hill or highest Wall   (<i>P.L.</i>, Book IV, ll. 181–2)

There are straightforward puns like that of the ravens in <i>Paradise Regained</i>: but these are rare in comparison with half-puns or jingles:

> Which tempted our attempt, and wrought our fall
> <div align="right">(<i>P.L.</i>, Book I, l. 642)</div>

>   and to begirt th' Almighty Throne
> Beseeching or besieging   (<i>P.L.</i>, Book V, ll. 865–6)

> Sole partner and sole part of all these joyes
> <div align="right">(<i>P.L.</i>, Book IV, l. 411)</div>

>   On the part of Heav'n
> Now alienated, distance, and distaste
> <div align="right">(<i>P.L.</i>, Book IX, ll. 8–9)</div>

>   hee to be aveng'd,
> And to repaire his numbers thus impair'd
> <div align="right">(<i>P.L.</i>, Book IX, ll. 143–4)</div>

There are instances in which a verbal flourish, sometimes empty enough in itself, is made to give interest or significance:

> Blest pair; and O yet happiest if ye seek
> No happier state, and know to know no more.
>> *(P.L., Book IV, ll. 775-6)*

> A chance but chance may lead where I may meet
> Some wandring Spirit of Heav'n
>> *(P.L., Book IV, ll. 530-1)*

>> wilt taste
> No pleasure, though in pleasure, solitarie.
>> *(P.L., Book VIII, ll. 401-2)*

> Wonder not, sovran Mistress, if perhaps
> Thou canst, who art sole Wonder,
>> *(P.L., Book IX, ll. 532-3)*

Certain Latinisms provide also a touch of surprise, of stimulating difficulty:

>> him who disobeyes
> Mee disobeyes, *(P.L., Book V, ll. 611-12)*

> Man is not whom to warne: *(P.L., Book XI, l. 773)*

The grotesque ingenuity of some climaxes plays its part:

> Thoughts, which how found they harbour in thy brest
> *Adam*, missthought of her to thee so dear?
>> *(P.L., Book IX, ll. 288-9)*

The following passage is a good example of several of these devices within a small compass: it reminds us that Milton's conversation was 'very satirical', and suggests that his armoury of puns and jingles was drawn upon most frequently when his poetry assumed that tone:

> To these that sober Race of Men, whose lives
> Religious titl'd them the Sons of God,
> Shall yeild up all thir virtue, all thir fame

Ignobly, to the traines and to the smiles
Of these fair Atheists, and now swim in joy,
(Erelong to swim at larg) and laugh; for which
The world erelong a world of tears must weepe.

(P.L., Book XI, ll. 617–23)

The humour of 'No fear lest dinner cool' and the irony
frequently used by Satan are other manifestations of this
vein in Milton's poetry. It is a mistake to regard them
as occasional and regrettable lapses from epic dignity.
Like the almost fantastic ingenuity which Adam displays in speaking to his Creator, and which Eve uses
in the face of temptation, they spring from the depths
of Milton's mind. When Pope observed that:

In quibbles angel and archangel join,
And God the Father turns a school-divine,

he said no more than anyone can see; but his view of
the relation of these oddities to Milton's total achievement was that of a superficial critic.

Milton has in fact made this form of interest so much
his own that it may seem supererogatory to search for
the origins of something so personal in his Italian
exemplars. Yet there are in Tasso's *Mondo Creato* some
passages which are exactly parallel to Milton's verbal
conceits; and Milton may well have regarded these as
giving him licence and authority to indulge in what
came to him so easily. Tasso has some curious instances
of playing upon words:

Ma delle piante ancor chi tace il pianto?
But of the plants once more who speaks not the plaint?

(Mondo Creato, Giornata Terza)

Non cupidigia, o fame infame d'oro
Not avarice, nor infamous famishment for gold

(Ibid., Giornata Quinta)

Altri son della mano a' vezzi avezzi
Others are skilled in the charms of the hand

(Ibid.)

Basta la vite solo a farci accorto
Di nostra vita
Even the vine alone shows us a sign
Of our own life   (Ibid., Giornata Terza)

The appearance of this kind of verbal conceit in both Tasso's and Milton's blank verse confirms the affiliation between these works of the two poets.[1]

We do not, however, form a complete impression of the kinship and the distinction between the styles of the two poets in this respect, unless we compare *Paradise Lost* also with the *Gerusalemme Liberata*; for it is in Tasso's masterpiece that the conceited qualities of his manner are revealed in all their flamboyancy. An analysis of this aspect of Tasso's poetry provides one of the most memorable passages of De Sanctis's *History of Italian Literature*:

Learned as he is, his poetic material is full of reminiscences, and he received his notions of the world not directly, but by way of books. He sets to work on his work, refines and sharpens images and conceits: a manner which he calls in its external mechanism *'parlare disgiunto'*; and which is a *'lavoro di tarsie'*, as Galilei said.[2]

The whole of this analysis is worth reading in connexion with the origins of Milton's style, although in Tasso the form of the *ottava rima* encourages the tendency to epigram and antithesis of an exaggerated kind

[1] Playing upon words, and more especially on proper names, was an established device in sonnets in Italian ever since Petrarch had alluded to Laura as a laurel-tree. This trick was given new life by the fashion for heroic and complimentary sonnets in the sixteenth century. Poets who exchanged sonnets with one another would pun upon the name of the recipient as often as they could.

[2] *Storia della Letteratura Italiana* (Bari, 1925), ii. 168.

and veils the affiliations with *Paradise Lost.* But De
Sanctis makes clear that this ingenuity in straining after
effect is of the essence of Tasso's conception of the
'magnificent' style:

> The imagination in its visions has always at its side a peda-
> gogue, who analyses and distinguishes with logical precision,
> as in:
>
> > *Sparsa è d'armi la terra, e l'armi sparse*
> > *Di sangue, e il sangue col sudor si mesce.*
> > Covered with arms the earth is, and th' arms
> > With blood, and blood with sweat is all enmixed.

The poet seeks too great a stress and distinctness, tries to give a
significance even to the insignificant; and he seeks this significance in intellectual relationships even when he disposes
already of the more powerful resources of imagery and of the
most violent emotional excitement, as in:

> > *O sasso amato ed onorato tanto,*
> > *Che dentro hai le mie fiamme e fuori il pianto!*
> > O stony tomb beloved and honoured so,
> > Bearing within my flames, without my woe!

With such play upon words and fancies Tancred laments and
Armida raves, and even in the desperation of her suicide makes
a very ingenious little speech to her weapons, and concludes:

> > *Sani piaga di stral piaga d'amore,*
> > *E sia la morte medicina al core!*[1]
> > May arrow wounds heal wounds of love that smart,
> > And death be the physician to my heart!

It may seem a far cry from Tasso's knights and en-
chantresses to the solemnities of *Paradise Lost,* but there
is a real connexion between the poetic tissue of the two
epics. The difference is that Milton's subject supported
much better the continual seeking after effect which
accompanied the idea of 'magnificence'; 'he chose a

---

[1] *Storia della Letteratura Italiana* (Bari, 1925,) ii. 168.

subject', as Dr. Johnson said, 'on which too much could not be said'. Milton's use of verbal conceits is also controlled by a more severe ideal of art ar.d by a powerful intellectual tension than is to be found in Tasso.[1]

VI

Considered simply as a machine, Milton's epic man/ ner, and in particular his diction, can be seen to fulfil Tasso's ideal more completely than any of Tasso's own essays in 'magnificence'. The differing imaginative powers of the two poets, the differing intellectual climates of the sixteenth century in Italy and the seventeenth century in England, no doubt contributed much to this result. But it is due also to the differing qualities of the two languages, at least at that stage in their development. English in the seventeenth century had fresher and richer resources and was in closer rela/ tion to contemporary life and thought than was literary Italian in the sixteenth century. Milton indeed desired 'to use English words in a foreign idiom' and his ideal of style was to remove his poetic diction from common usage; but, despite these dangerous ambitions, he had behind him, and he freely drew upon, the vigorous freedom of Elizabethan English. In contrast, poets in Italy in the sixteenth century, whether or not they were Tuscans (and Tasso was Neapolitan by birth and

[1] Verbal cleverness, grotesqueness, and obscurity are perhaps more essential features of epic poetry, or all high poetry, than our critical tradition has always admitted. The 'kennings' of Anglo-Saxon and Scandinavian verse are no more incompatible with 'high seriousness' than Shakespeare's conceits or Dante's constant and sometimes play- ful circumlocutions. Perhaps Milton's verbal wit and logic-chopping give his epic some qualities akin to these and safeguard it from the perils of neo-classical decorum by breathing into it a primitive or personal zest.

Ferrarese by adoption), had to write their serious poetry in the dialect of Dante and Petrarch. This literary language, which had been fresh two centuries before, had in their time been carefully refined and codified, so that Della Casa's *Galateo*, for example, is a masterpiece of prose style, but of the prose style of the fourteenth century. Tasso was attempting to impose an artificial diction on a literary language already burdened by exacting demands of grammar and idiom.

The variety of linguistic resources which might have helped to support epic 'magnificence' was therefore lacking in Italian at this time, and Tasso's blank verse in particular is made of a more monotonous substance, and has a smaller range of verbal harmonies and contrasts, than Milton's. No doubt this also has something to do with permanent differences in the structure and texture of the two languages. The vocabulary of English is less polysyllabic than that of Italian, yet it can offer its Latin element for polysyllabic effects if they are desired; and the greater proportion of monosyllables and the relative lack of inflexions enable the English poet to achieve effects of bareness and simplicity which add greatly to this total range. This is in part a matter of taste. Effects of bareness and simplicity seem to have appealed little to Tasso, while Milton consciously reserves them for some of the finest moments of his poem. But this contrast between the manners of the two poets corresponds also to a contrast between the substances of their native tongues.

8

MILTON'S BLANK VERSE:
THE PROSODY

I

THE distinction between a poet's diction and his prosody is arbitrary. The artistic purpose of a poem cannot be apprehended except through the structure of its verse; it is embodied in the arrangement of the words, whether these are considered as sense or as sound, and Tasso's account of the 'magnificent' style rightly took metrical devices in its stride. The *asprezza* he desired might be obtained, so he thought, not only in a complex diction (*parlar disgiunto*), but in weighty rhythms, and certain conjunctions of vowels and consonants, sometimes in the body of the line, sometimes at the end.

The same interdependence of sense and sound is Milton's aim. Miltonic prosody cannot be understood independently of Miltonic diction. However, it may be admitted that we feel there is a practical distinction to be made between the arrangement of words in any specific passage and the presumed metrical pattern to which they belong: that is to say, many arrangements of words in a specific poem can only be read aright as 'words for music', and the music to which they are to be sung in *Paradise Lost* is the '*English* Heroic Verse without Rime'.[1] This experience of Milton's verse is

[1] Milton's note on the verse of *Paradise Lost*.

the justification for treating the metrical questions here as a part, yet a distinguishable part, of the subject of Milton's epic style.

II

There is a clear connexion between Milton's prosodic system in his epic blank verse and the recommendations made by Tasso in the *Discorsi*.

Tasso's verbal devices which approximate to prosodic features are:

I. The clogging of the verse by means of accumulated consonants.

II. The conjunction of open vowels, which may be of two kinds, either (*a*) elided, or (*b*) unelided.

III. The use of double consonants in the penultimate syllables of the line.

Milton could hope to apply these with varying degrees of success in English.

I. Milton is not afraid to clog his lines with many and harsh consonants if he desires to obtain a sensation of almost physical unpleasantness or difficulty:

> greedily they pluck'd
> The frutage fair to sight, like that which grew
> Neer that bituminous Lake where *Sodom* flam'd;
> This more delusive, not the touch, but taste
> Deceav'd; they fondly thinking to allay
> Thir appetite with gust, instead of Fruit
> Chewd bitter Ashes, which th' offended taste
> With spattering noise rejected: oft they assayd,
> Hunger and thirst constraining, drugd as oft,
> With hatefullest disrelish, writh'd thir jaws
> With soot and cinders fill'd;
>
> (*P.L.*, Book X, ll. 560–70)

In general, however, Milton does not need to seek this effect with such deliberation as an Italian poet would, for the more consonantal substance of English makes this type of harshness more difficult to avert than to achieve.

II. The highly vowelled nature of Italian gives especial scope for these collocations, especially of elided vowels. (*a*) What Milton did was to try to introduce this effect into English not only in its simplest form, but by allowing a similar so-called elision where a vowel is conjoined with certain other sounds, mainly liquid consonants. The simplest form is to be found everywhere in his blank verse:

> in thee,
> Not in themselves, all thir known vertue appeers
>> (*P.L.*, Book IX, l. 110)

> Our dayes work brought to little, though begun
> Early, and th' hour of Supper comes unearn'd.
>> (*P.L.*, Book IX, ll. 224-5)

Of the various elisions he devises to extend this effect the best examples are given by Robert Bridges.[1] One may cite, to make clear the type of elision meant:

> Carnation, Purple, Azure, or spect with Gold,
>> (*P.L.*, Book IX, l. 429)

> Of good, how just? if evil, if what is evil
> Be real, why not known, since easier shunnd?
>> (*P.L.*, Book IX, ll. 698-9)

> How dies the Serpent? hee hath eat'n and lives,
>> (*P.L.*, Book IX, l. 764)

Bridges points out that the term 'elision' is not strictly applicable in cases like these where none of the sounds

---

[1] *Milton's Prosody* (Oxford, 1921), pp. 26-37.

are meant to be suppressed or lost.[1] The purpose and effect of these colliding sounds cannot be understood except as Milton's equivalent for the coming together of open vowels in Italian; there, too, in the cases meant by Tasso, neither of the vowels is suppressed or lost, but rather they glide into one another, giving an effect of indescribable suspense and fullness to the verse:

> O de' mortali
> Egri conforto, obblio dolce de' mali
> Sì gravi, onde è la vita aspra e noiosa.
>
> (Della Casa, Sonetto L)

(b) The collocation of open vowels where they do not, as Tasso says, 'swallow each other', is, as a specially noticeable effect, practically confined to Italian, for in English it is too common to be made much of.

> Là onde il carro già era sparito

is a striking line, embodying a kind of gulf, a sensation of emptiness. Perhaps a faint echo of this effect may be heard in these lines:

> Yet not till the Creator from his work
> Desisting, though unwearied, up returnd
> Up to the Heav'n of Heav'ns his high abode,
> Thence to behold this new created World
> Th' addition of his Empire, how it shew'd
> In prospect from his Throne, how good, how faire,
> Answering his great Idea. Up he rode
> Followd with acclamation
>
> (P.L., Book VII, ll. 551-8)

But on the whole this device makes too little impression in English to be used on a large scale.

---

[1] Milton's Prosody (Oxford, 1921), p. 9.

III. It has already been suggested that Tasso's mania for double consonants in the last syllables of his verses may have had some effect on the tone or tune of Milton's blank verse.[1] The device could not of course be imitated precisely in English; and since the 'English Heroic Verse' is not hendecasyllabic but decasyllabic, there is not quite the same need to strengthen the tenth syllable. It may be, however, that Tasso's practice made Milton feel that the tenth syllable of his line must be its pivot, and must therefore be capable at least of receiving a strong stress when it did not demand one. Milton very seldom ends a line with such words as 'modesty', 'amity', 'misery'. Reading his blank verse with attention to the line-endings reveals that he prefers a good long vowel or a marked consonantal ending. This preference seems to solve the question of how to read such lines as:

> Beyond all past example and future,
> (*P.L.*, Book X, l. 840)

This exigency also corresponds to what Bridges expressed in other terms when he came to the conclusion that Milton had 'freed' every 'foot' in his blank verse line except the last.[2]

III

It has always been recognized that Milton wrote his epic blank verse to some prosodic system; but no attempt was made to examine his practice and to define his rules until that made over a period of more

[1] See p. 41.
[2] See the Note on Neo-Miltonics in *Collected Essays XI, XII, XIII, XIV, XV*, p. 87. But this observation is blurred in *Milton's Prosody* (Oxford, 1921), pp. 39–42.

than thirty years by Robert Bridges.[1] In the final edition
of his essay Bridges wrote:

My purpose in writing these notes on Milton was to draw
attention to his workmanship, and on the evidence of his prosody ensure that his verse should be read rightly. It is a common
opinion that there is no such thing as English prosody; and
most of our classical scholars have regarded the ten-syllable
verses of Chaucer, Shakespeare, and Milton, as so many better
or worse attempts to compose regular, alternately stressed so-
called iambic lines, broken here and there by the negligent
admission of 'superfluous' syllables.[2]

But the method which Bridges adopted at first and retained even in the last revision of his study did not attack
the traditional assumption with sufficient boldness;
and it is apparent to the careful reader that Bridges came
to see this, and phrased his final account of Milton's
blank verse in such a way as to show that he had deep
mental reservations concerning his method of analysis.

The beginning of his study suggests that he considers what is to follow as the results of a working
hypothesis only:

In this treatise the scheme adopted for the examination of
Milton's matured prosody in the blank verse of *Paradise Lost* is
to assume a normal regular line, and tabulate all the variations
as exceptions to that norm.

For this purpose English blank verse may conveniently be
regarded as a decasyllabic line on a disyllabic basis and in rising
rhythm (i.e. with accents or stresses on the alternate even
syllables); and the disyllabic units may be called *feet*.[3]

He adds a footnote distinguishing between 'accentual
blank verse' and 'syllabic verse': it is clear that he con-

[1] *Milton's Prosody*, Revised Final Edition (Oxford, 1921). The
history of the book is given in Note A, p. 113, in this edition.
[2] Ibid., pp. 83–84.   [3] Ibid., p. 1.

siders Milton's blank verse to be of the latter kind, yet he says 'the rhythmical basis of syllabic blank verse has never been satisfactorily determined, nor will it be dis-cussed in this book'.[1]

What Bridges has done, therefore, is to concede to the traditional view that English prosody must be inter-preted in terms of Classical prosody. This is what he concedes in regarding the decasyllabic line as 'on a disyllabic basis and in rising rhythm', and calling 'the disyllabic units' feet. It is precisely these conceptions which have weighed most heavily on all theories of English prosody. The fact that Bridges's study is a most illuminating account of Milton's practice does not re-deem its fundamentally false assumptions. It could not but show readers that Milton's practice was systematic, in tabulating verses which were supposed irregular but which could be shown to confine so-called irregularity within certain limits. But something is clearly wrong when Bridges has to declare, as he does in the earlier stages of his description, that 'Milton came to scan his verses in one way, and to read them in another'.[2]

Elsewhere Bridges indicates clearly the direction in which he came to see that he should have looked. 'There can be little doubt', he says in a note, 'that Milton's admiration of Dante's rich rhythms was the main cause of his own: and that he sought to improve our English verse by the same accentual variety.'[3] And in considering the difficulties of reducing to rule the variety of rhythms in 'syllabic blank verse' he concludes that 'in such a laborious investigation, the tabulation of Milton's and Dante's rhythms should offer the best groundwork'.[4] The prosodist's ear has informed him, it seems, that there is a close affinity between the

[1] Ibid., p. 1, note 1. [2] Ibid., p. 35.
[3] Note C, p. 115. [4] Ibid., p. 38.

structure of the Italian hendecasyllable, as it appears in Dante, and Milton's 'English Heroic Verse'. But he regards this as no simplification of his problem, but rather as an additional complication; and indeed it is, if it is to be dealt with by his method of painstaking tabulation of 'inversions' in various 'feet', variations from one falsely assumed norm. The value of Milton's adaptation of Italian verse is that it enables us to dis-pense with all these impositions of arbitrary rules, and to read the verse, as Milton wrote it, with a basis of very few fixed principles.

That Milton thoroughly understood the basis of Italian prosody is obvious from his own sonnets in Italian, and these contain analogues to many of the lines which, when they occur in his English blank verse, give such trouble to Bridges and his friends.[1] There is no reason to suppose that Milton had only Dante's rhythms in mind in his emulation of Tuscan in English. Dante is for a hundred good reasons the poet whose power impresses itself most on a modern English reader, and whose style overwhelms us with its combination of living colloquial idiom and poetic art. But there is no evidence that Milton shared our pre-ference of Dante's style to that of the other Tuscan poets

[1] For example:

> M'accostandosi attorno, e perchè scrivi (Canzone)
> Diodati, e te'l dirò con maraviglia (Sonnet IV)
> Di timori, e speranze al popol use (Sonnet VI)

are of the type of Italian rhythm Milton is echoing in:

And Tiresias and Phineus prophets old. (P.L., Book III, l. 36).

He effected; Man he made, and for him built (P.L., Book IX, l. 152).

Into utter darkness, deep ingulft, his place (P.L., Book V, l. 614).

Landor has related these rhythms to Italian poetry in his remarks on Milton in The Poems of Catullus, where he says: '. . . there is no verse whatsoever in any of his poems for the metre of which he has not an Italian prototype.'

he knew; and there is much evidence that he admired the style of some of those others to the degree of imitating it as closely as he could. Now, since the structure of the verse of these other Tuscan poets is at bottom the same as that of Dante's, it would seem to follow that Milton derived his notions of rhythmic strength and beauty quite as much from the study of these writers—Petrarch, Della Casa, and Tasso—as from the *Divine Comedy*.

From our present point of view the great interest of this adoption of Italian models is that it made un-necessary the construction of any such system of pro-sody as that which Robert Bridges attempted and which is generally considered indispensable by scholars. For Dante himself, in the *De Vulgari Eloquentia*, made no such attempt, confining himself to a list of the differ-ing lengths of line that could be used and of the stanza forms in which they were best used. His formulation was a mere indication, illustrated by examples which he evidently thought quite adequately clear in them-selves. And at no time, either in the fourteenth or six-teenth centuries, did Italian poets think it necessary to give any essentially different account. Tasso, in *La Cavalletta ovvero Della Poesia Toscana*, concerns himself with much detailed analysis of the forms of Tuscan verse, the structure and use of the *canzone*, the madrigal, and the *ballata*, but pays no more heed to the rhythmic or syllabic pattern of the verses than his predecessors.

The explanation of this happy immunity from pro-sodic theory is not far to seek. Tuscan poetry had achieved formal mastery in the early fourteenth cen-tury, well before the Revival of Learning which came to full flower at the turn of the *Quattrocento*. The pres-tige of Greek and Latin might overwhelm for a time the reputation of Dante and Petrarch, but at no time was there any danger that Greek and Latin prosody might be applied to the structure of their verse; for at no time was anyone foolish enough to suppose that it might be relevant.[1]

There is no need to trace the origins of the *dolce stil nuovo* in Provence or Sicily to see that its highly developed technique was firmly based on rhyme and music. The emancipation from musical accompaniment made possible Dante's verse; the achievement of Dante and Petrarch established Tuscan, if not as the 'illustrious cardinal, courtly and curial' language which Dante had sought,[2] as the most polished vernacular in Europe. The body of beautiful and profound poetry in this language by the end of the fourteenth century enabled it to impose its own technique and standards of excellence for many generations to come. Bembo might have to come to its defence more than a century later; a humanist like Ercole Strozzi might doubt whether it was possible to distinguish good writing from bad in the vulgar tongue.[3] But there was really no doubt about it: Dante, Petrarch, and Boccaccio had provided masterpieces which could not be denied, and examples enough to enable later poets to learn how to produce exquisite verse entirely without the aid of any expressed system of prosody.

That Tuscan poetry had principles of structure which might be said to constitute a prosody cannot, of course, be denied; but, while some of these were essential and were therefore stated from the beginning, others (and those the ones which are especially relevant to Milton's blank verse) were scarcely ever stated, because in practice their effects were infinitely various and could be

[1] Claudio Tolomei and others in the sixteenth century attempted to devise Italian equivalents of Classical metres, but made no attempt to explain existing Italian verse in Classical terms.

[2] *De Vulgari Eloquentia*, Book I, chapter xvii.

[3] See p. 8.

left, in the hands of a competent poet, to look after themselves.

Thus Dante points to two elements only, the length of the line and the pattern of rhymes in the *canzone*.[1] He omits entirely any consideration of stress, the licensed variety of which is a distinctive feature of his own and all later Italian verse. It is plain that the wonderful variety of his rhythms came to him from instinct, in working out the possibilities of his form and his language. His form is the *terza rima*, that is, a stanza of three lines: the rhyme pattern is emphasized, not disguised, and therefore the penultimate syllable of the line is always stressed. The line is of eleven theoretic syllables, but the vowelled nature of the language makes 'elision' particularly easy and variety of rhythm very great. What results is a line almost, but not quite, released from all obligations of stress except the stress on the penultimate syllable: for it was found that one other stress must be, if not fixed, at least limited in its freedom. Bembo, himself one of the most accomplished verse-makers of his period, states this rule casually in the *Prose*:

For since, in order to form the verse it is required of necessity that the accents should be in the fourth or the sixth and in the tenth syllable; every time that, however it may be, it does not possess one of these two placings (of the accent), it is no longer a verse, whatever is the state of the other syllables. And this may be said no less of the broken (i.e. shorter) verse than of the whole verse, in so far as it is capable of receiving the accent.[2]

[1] *De Vulgari Eloquentia*, Book II, chapters ix–xiii.
[2] 'Che conciossiacosachè a formare il verso necessariamente si richiegga, che nella quarta, o nella sesta, e nella decima sillaba siano sempre gli accenti; ogni volta, che qualunque si è, l'una di queste due positure non gli ha, quello non è più verso, comunque poi si stiano le altre sillabe. E questo detto sia non meno del verso rotto, che dello intero, in quanto ello capevole ne può essere.' *Prose* (Verona, 1743),

The *Cinquecento* was the century of Greek and Latin pedantry, and of a series of Italian critics who tried to apply the heritage of Greek and Latin rhetoric to their own literature. Then, if ever, one might have expected an attempt to impose Classical prosody on the Tuscan form of verse. But the attempt was not made, for the plain reason that Tuscan poetry was quite sufficiently provided with a prosodic basis of its own. The latinization of the vulgar tongue affected style and diction, and eventually introduced new forms of verse, notably *versi sciolti*: but these new forms were based upon the old prosody, with its flexible but strictly governed combination of stress and syllable.

IV

Milton in his exploration of Italian poetry thus became expert in a large and varied body of verse raised upon the foundations of a vernacular prosody antedating the Revival of Learning, and unaffected in its essentials by the ever more ambitious attempts of the Italians to emulate Classical literature. In making his own attempt to 'overgo' Virgil and Homer (and, of course, Ariosto and Tasso and Spenser) he therefore had no need to devise a theory of prosody: his literary genius and his linguistic instinct sufficed him in his task of adapting Italian epic diction and verse to English.

p. 93. Bembo gives two examples of how moving an accent from the fourth or sixth place can destroy the rhythm of a line.

   Voi, ch'ascoltate in rime sparse il suono (Petrarch, Sonnet 1)
and
   Per fare una leggiadra sua vendetta (Ibid., Sonnet 11)
cease to be verses if we write:
   Voi, ch'in rime sparse ascoltate il suono
and
   Per far una sua leggiadra vendetta.

He did not try to reproduce Italian rhythms exactly and for their own sake; he sought to find their equivalent, as far as it might be found, in English. The result is a new and unmistakable movement in the verse, which is at once bolder and stronger, and yet more fixed and, as it were, solidified, than any previous verse in English. Its laws are simply an equivalent of the principles underlying the Italian hendecasyllable, and may be summarized as:

I. The line has a theoretic ten syllables (not eleven, as in Italian).

II. The tenth syllable must always have, or be capable of being given, a stress; one other stress must fall, in any one line, on either the fourth or the sixth syllable.

The elisions possible in English to increase the number of real, as opposed to theoretic, syllables, Milton found to be fewer than in Italian; and, as a consequence of this (for in Italian it is the incidence of elision which most violently shifts the stresses), the variety of his rhythms is not so great in practice as their theoretic liberty. To place against the relatively more limited capacities of English for this kind of verse, Milton has one enormous advantage: the more consonantal and monosyllabic substance of his language makes the texture of his verse more varied than that of Italian, whether in the direction of simplicity or that of rich compression.

This account of the matter will be found to cover all the phenomena of Milton's blank verse; and where a simpler explanation will cover the facts, there is no reason to prefer to it a more complex, such as that given by Robert Bridges. The chief motive of these more elaborate theories is a desire to make of Milton's prosody (and by implication of English prosody as such) something that it is not: a system of rules as abstractly rigid as those which scholars conceive to have operated in Greek and Latin poetry.[1]

Bridges himself was a practising poet with a fine ear, and he was too perceptive and expert to accept whole-heartedly the demands he was expected to satisfy; but he was unfortunately prepared to betray his own per-ceptions, and to give pleasurable exercise to his in-genuity, by devising structures in which he had no real faith.[2]

[1] The sign of this attempt is always the introduction of the notion of 'feet' into metrical analysis: only so, it is felt, can every stress and syllable of the verse be subjected to rule. But in English verse such 'feet' do not exist, any more than they do in French or Italian. The metrical unit is, for example, in the decasyllable, the line itself, with all its possible variations, not the five 'disyllabic feet' which are said to compose it.

[2] A comparison between the earlier and the later editions of *Milton's Prosody* will make clear the wavering and ambiguous quality of Robert Bridges's judgements. In the edition of 1893, Appendix G, 'On the Use of Greek Terminology in English Pro-sody', was a plain rejection of that tradition: it does not appear in the final edition. Appendix E in 1893 quoted Tyrwhitt as an example of the blunderings of English scholars in trying to define the nature of English verse rhythms: 'On the tenth (or rhyming) syllable a strong accent is in all cases indispensably required, and in order to make the line tolerably harmonious, it seems necessary that at least *two more* of the even syllables should be accented, the *fourth* being (almost always) one of them.' In 1921 Bridges adds a com-ment which begins by confirming the inadequacy of this description, but ends by suggesting that Tyrwhitt's remarks do nevertheless con-tain the root of the matter.

It may be pointed out that Tyrwhitt's account of the English decasyllable comes very near to that given above, as coming to Milton from the Italians.

9

THE CHORUSES OF
SAMSON AGONISTES

I

THE choruses of *Samson Agonistes* are most often discussed from what may be called the strictly prosodic point of view. Robert Bridges, though with a characteristic glance at those he was trying to satisfy, said that 'if I enable the reader to scan the verses, and, if he choose, count and name the metrical units, I may expect that he will then feel himself free to admire the rhythms';[1] and accordingly set out to give 'an account of the elemental structure of the verse of *Samson Agonistes*'.[2] The curious variety of rhythms, and the unexpected and constantly varied lengths of the verses, are what indeed must strike us as requiring explanation; but, as in the blank verse of *Paradise Lost*, the prosody cannot be completely distinguished from the diction and the total structure of the poetry. What we have, first and last, is an arrangement of certain words in a specific passage of a specific work of art. Thus the rhythms of the choruses in *Samson* cannot be considered except as combined with the use of rhyme, the constant suggestion of lyrical stanzas; and the whole effect must be seen in relation to the dramatic structure of the poem. These lyrical passages are speeches; some of

[1] *Milton's Prosody* (Oxford, 1893), p. 33.   [2] Ibid.

them are monodies for the chief person of the drama, the rest are commentaries on his situation and actions.

It may be said at once that there is no precise parallel in Italian poetry to all the prosodic features of the choruses; and it is impossible that, within the limits of traditional Italian prosody, there could have been any such parallel. But even with this reservation the choruses may at least be placed in relation to certain Italian examples, as well as in relation to Milton's own development or adaptation of the Italian heroic manner. The novel prosodic basis may be seen as Milton's equivalent in English for a variety of effects which were possible in Italian within different metrical limits. And these are part of a total effect which is quite plainly related to certain Italian lyrical dramas of the sixteenth century. We have, moreover, Milton's own word for it that there is a connexion with Italian Renaissance drama: 'That *Chorus* is here introduc'd after the Greek manner, not antient only but modern, and still in use among the *Italians*. In the modelling therefore of this Poem, with good reason, the Antients and *Italians* are rather follow'd, as of much more authority and fame.'[1] It is true that when Milton passes to 'the measure of Verse us'd in the Chorus' he refers to Greek example only; but it is difficult to believe that Italian experiments did not play here too the part they had usually played in his emulation of the Classics.

II

To find the clue to the structure of Milton's choruses one must turn to Tasso's *Aminta* and Guarini's *Pastor Fido*. These two pastoral dramas are very different from

[1] See the Preface to *Samson Agonistes*.

Milton's tragedy in their atmosphere and aim and effect. But Milton was not, after all, prejudiced against the artifices of pastoral poetry; and these two plays were not only the acknowledged masterpieces of Italian pastoral, they were among the most famous and admired works of the age. And they would not have been so if they had not in some sort deserved it; in both, but particularly in Tasso's poem, there circulates a breath of living poetic imagination, which, whether or not we can explain or justify it, communicates itself through all their absurdities and unrealities. It is not at all unlikely that Milton felt their peculiar charm intensely in his youth, and recalled their technical mastery when he came, in his old age, to write his own very different drama.

Certainly the technique of *Aminta* and the *Pastor Fido* cannot be dissociated entirely from that of the Italian tragedies of the Renaissance; the use of blank verse dialogue and the imitation of the Greek chorus is much the same in all the learned drama of the period. But no breath of poetic life circulates in the joyless regions of Italian tragedy; Tasso in *Torrismondo* convinces us as little as Trissino in *Sofonisba*, or Ludovico Dolce in his imitations of Euripides. Milton might regard with respect the sustained polish of *Torrismondo* or *Sofonisba*; but between these and his own powerful use of the form of Greek tragedy, something has intervened, and that is the more organic, more spontaneous, form of lyrical drama found in *Aminta*, and Guarini's imitation of it.

One of the signs of the greater vitality of these two plays is precisely their use of the chorus; this is more highly developed in the later play, but in both one finds the first unmistakable appearance of the form of chorus 'call'd by the Greeks *Monostrophic*, or rather

Apolelymenon, without regard had to *Strophe, Anti-strophe* or *Epod'*.[1]

The choruses of *Sofonisba* were constructed to the Greek pattern of strophe, antistrophe, and epode, each of these units employing the rhymed stanzaic methods of the Italian *canzone*; at the end of the Fourth Act the chorus sings a strophe and antistrophe each of sixteen lines, followed by an epode made up of two stanzas, one of eleven lines, the other of seven. This is followed by a long antiphonal chorus, in which a courtier and the chorus sing alternately eight lines, the second eight lines rhyming with the first eight.[2] These eight-line units having been repeated eight times, the chorus concludes with an epode of twelve lines, the first of which is, in the manner of the *commiato* to a *canzone*, unrhymed:

> *O misera Regina*
> *Mentre, che t'apparecchi a fare honore*
> *Al nuovo sposo, harai nuovo dolore.*
> *O che dura ambasciata sarà quella,*
> *Che ti dirà, ch'al campo*
> *Vadi, per esser serva de' Romani.*
> *Lassa, pensando di disdegno avampo,*
> *Ch'una donna sì bella*

---

[1] Preface to *Samson Agonistes.* Milton uses these terms also to describe the form of his Latin poem to John Rouse, written in 1646, and published in 1673, in the second edition of the *Poems.* A Latin note to the poem explains that although the verses are divided into strophes, antistrophes, and epode, these divisions are not accurate, since there is no repeated pattern. Milton adds, '. . . it had been more proper, perhaps, to call this sort of writing "monostrophic". The metres are, in part, κατὰ σχέσιν, i.e. in correlation, responsive, in part ἀπολελυμένα, i.e. free from such restraint of correlation' (translation from *The Poetical Works of John Milton* (Oxford, 1938), Appendix II, p. 605). It would be interesting to know whether Latin verses of this kind originated in seventeenth-century Italy, suggested by the development of free lyric forms from the *canzone.*

[2] The rhyme scheme is thus a stanza of sixteen lines:
a b c d e f g h / a b c d e f g h.

Divenga preda in sì feroci mani.
O dio, fa, che sian vani
Questi nostri sospetti, ahi, che vien fuore
Serva, che piange, e si distrugge il cuore.[1]

The Servant then enters and the Fifth Act begins.

In Tasso's *Torrismondo* the choruses which conclude each Act are immeasurably richer in poetic ornament, the ornaments of 'magnificence', than those in *Sofonisba*; but they are, in their own fashion, no less mechanically constructed. Tasso uses repeated stanzas, put together in the manner of *canzoni*, and concludes his choruses, as *canzoni* were concluded, with a few rhymed lines (the first may be unrhymed), a fragment of stanza, a kind of dying fall or terse dismissal.

Only in the concluding choruses of these two tragedies do we find examples of what Milton calls monostrophic choruses: these are brief, in accordance with Greek example, and restrained in rhetoric and emotion. That from *Torrismondo* is perhaps the most memorable passage from that unfortunate drama:

CORO

Ahi lagrime! ahi dolore!
Passa la vita, e si dilegua, e fugge,
Come gel, che si strugge.
Ogni altezza s'inchina, e sparge a terra
Ogni fermo sostegno:
Ogni possente regno

[1] 'O wretched Queen, while thou prepar'st to do honour to thy new spouse, thou shalt have a new sorrow. O what a hard message will that be which tells thee thou art to go to the camp to be slave to the Romans. Alas, in thinking of it I flame with indignation, that so lovely a lady should become a prey to such cruel hands. O God, may these our fears be vain: ah, now comes forth a servant, weeping and racked by grief.' *La Sofonisba, Tragedia di M. Giovan Giorgio Trissino* (Venice, 1535), p. 28.

In pace cadde alfin, se crebbe in guerra.
E come raggio il verno, imbruna, e muore
Gloria, d'altrui splendore.
E come alpestro, e rapido torrente,
Come acceso baleno
In notturno sereno,
Come aura, o fumo, o come stral repente,
Volan le nostre fame, ed ogni onore
Sembra languido fiore.
    Che più si spera, o che s'attende omai?
Dopo trionfo, e palma
Sol qui restano all' alma
Lutto, e lamenti, e lagrimosi lai.
Che più giova Amicizia, o giova Amore?
Ahi lagrime! ahi dolore![1]

In such a relatively compressed lyric as this there is a certain anticipation of Milton's manner in some of the choruses of *Samson*. One cannot understand Milton's form without comparing it to these sixteenth-century tragedies; but the pastoral dramas exhibit a stage of lyrical writing which is nearer still to the English.

Tasso in the choruses of the *Aminta* makes, indeed, few formal innovations. In the most memorable of all, that which sums up the mood of the play, *O bel età dell' oro*,[2]

---

[1] *Chorus.* 'Ah tears, ah sorrow! Life passes, and is scattered, and flees, like ice which destroys itself. Every majesty bows down, and every firm support is cast down to earth: every powerful kingdom falls at last in time of peace, if it grew in war. And like sunlight in winter, glory grows dull and dies in others' splendour. And like a steep and rapid stream, like lightning kindled in a night-sky, like air, or smoke, or a swift arrow, our fame flies, and every honour seems but a languishing flower.

'What more may be hoped for, or what henceforth can be expected? After victory and garlands here there remain for the soul but grief and lamentings and tearful songs. What now avails Friendship, what avails Love? Ah tears, ah sorrow!' *Opere*, vol. ii, *Il Torrismondo*, p. 128.

[2] Ibid., *Aminta*, p. 36.

he uses the form of the *canzone*. But in the briefer choruses which conclude the other Acts he uses the monostrophic form; and in the least perfunctory of these, that at the end of the Second Act and that at the end of the Fifth, there is a loosening of the rhyme scheme, a proportion of unrhymed lines, which is a development in the direction of *Samson*, and significant in itself of a new manner in Tasso's own poetry, the peculiar formula of Italian pastoral drama.

For the lyrical passages in *Aminta* are not confined to the choruses; they occur throughout the dialogue, and the delightful smoothness with which the regular blank verse passes into semi-lyrical verse, unrhymed or partly rhymed, makes one of the principal charms of the play. Strictly speaking, it is not a play but an eclogue, and this gives the key to its lyric manner. A spectator of the original performance refers to it thus, and points to the introduction of the chorus between the Acts as a novelty, which it would surely not have been accounted in a work of which the origin was a desire to imitate classical drama.[1]

The choruses in *Aminta* are therefore but an extension, an intensification, of the lyrical qualities inherent in the speeches, and which flower so easily into idyllic pictures or flights of emotion. In the First Act we have two such lyrical dialogues, one in which Daphne tries to dissuade Silvia from too cruel a chastity; the other in which Thyrsis receives the confidences of Amyntas. When Daphne urges that love is in accordance with

[1] The 'Eclogue', this spectator reports from Ferrara early in 1574, 'è stata tenuta per una delle più vaghe composizioni, che siano finora uscite in scena in tal genere . . . e quello che di grazia s'è aggiunto a questa Egloga, e ch'ha piaciuto più che mediocremente, è la novità del Coro fra ciascuno Atto, che rendeva maestà mirabile, e recava con piacevolissimi concetti diletto agli spettatori ed ascoltatori'. *Opere*, vol. ii, *Aminta*, p. 5.

the persuasions of Nature, the blank verse passes into
a form of chant:

> *Mira là quel colombo*
> *Con che dolce sussurro lusingando*
> *Bacia la sua compagna:*
> *Odi quell' usignuolo,*
> *Che va di ramo in ramo*
> *Cantando: Io amo, io amo: e, se nol sai,*
> *La biscia or lascia il suo veleno, e corre*
> *Cupida al suo amatore:*
> *Van le tigre in amore:*
> *Ama il leon superbo: e tu sol, fiera*
> *Più che tutte le fere,*
> *Albergo gli dineghi nel tuo petto.*[1]

When Amyntas enters lamenting Silvia's indifference,
and when he recounts to Thyrsis the birth of his love
for her, the dialogue moves into the same region of
floating song-like speech. *Aminta* is therefore an extended eclogue, or lyrical drama, in which Tasso revealed new possibilities to Italian verse. When Guarini
took up the form and exploited its capacities for
artificial and ornate musicality, he developed precisely
these innovations of Tasso. In the *Pastor Fido* a far
greater proportion of the dialogue is written in the
semi-lyrical measure, with its basis of heptasyllables:
the lengthy Prologue is a good example. And of
Guarini's elaborate choruses, three are written in the
monostrophic form which is distinguished from the
semi-lyrical dialogues only by being rhymed through-

---

[1] 'Look under at that dove, which wooing with sweet murmurs
kisses his companion: hear yonder nightingale, which goes from
bough to bough singing: *I love, I love*: and, lest thou know it not,
the viper now forsakes her venom and runs desirous to her lover:
tigers are moved by love: the proud lion loves: and thou alone,
more fierce than all the beasts, deny'st him shelter in thy breast.'
Opere, vol. ii, *Aminta*, p. 21.

out.[1] The *Pastor Fido* is inferior to *Aminta* in charm, perhaps because of the more thoroughgoing efficiency with which the notion of a pastoral drama is exploited; but this very efficiency exhibits the formal basis more clearly, and the monostrophic choruses of Guarini emerge as one of the most brilliant features of his play.

III

When we consider the severely logical dramatic and metrical construction of Milton's drama as a whole, we can have little doubt that it has close affinities only with the more disciplined of the Italian poetic dramas:[2] that is why *Sofonisba* and *Aminta* and *Il Pastor Fido*, polished and concentrated as they are, can contribute to our understanding of Milton's methods. But it is necessary to consider also a very differently organized dramatic poem, *L'Adamo* of Andreini, for this too is related in some degree to the technical innovations made by Tasso and Guarini, and there is no doubt that Milton knew it, and was even much impressed by it; his first sketch of a drama on the subject of *Paradise Lost*, which he called *Adam Unparadised*, shows the influence of Andreini's *sacra rappre-sentazione*.

L'Adamo, printed in 1617, is a specimen of the Counter-Reformation development of the medieval

---

[1] Of the other two choruses, one is a *canzone*, the other alludes to Tasso's *O bel età dell' oro* by taking the same subject and using, not only the same stanza, but even the same rhyme-words, as the original.

[2] The tragedies of Federigo della Valle (1560?–1628), published in 1626–7, use Tasso's and Guarini's free form of chorus. The example from *Ester*, given in *The Oxford Book of Italian Verse* (Oxford, 1952), pp. 242–4, shows a certain affinity with Milton's choruses.

miracle-play. It is at bottom an allegorical pageant and opera, and has no real dramatic kinship either with Italian imitations of Greek tragedy or with the pastoral drama descended from Classical eclogues. But Andreini adopted for his dialogue and his choruses the metrical liberties introduced by Tasso and Guarini. Since his work is a lyrical or semi-lyrical spectacle, he uses for dialogue a combination of long and short lines, hendecasyllables and heptasyllables, luxuriantly irregular in arrangement and embellished here and there with rhyme. For his choruses he has the same combination of long and short lines, disposed with the same irregularity, but rhymed throughout (or almost, for occasionally a line is left unrhymed).[1]

The derivation of this lyrical rhetoric from *Il Pastor Fido* is clear. But the formal discipline, or indiscipline, of this religious drama can have been of little use to so fastidious an artist as Milton. The metrical freedom established by Tasso's and Guarini's pastoral dramas was seized upon by second-rate poets like Marino and third-rate poets like Andreini, and exploited with all the facility at their disposal. The result is often temporarily dazzling, as an exhibition of rhetorical and metrical skill: *L'Adamo* is impressive in its sustained pomp and showy artifice, though its poetry is scarcely of a kind that can bear close examination.[2]

However, its possible connexion with *Samson Agonistes* can be summed up briefly enough. Both its monostrophic choruses and its use of intermittent

---

[1] In a few instances (see Scenes IV and V of Act III) he introduces small regularly rhymed choruses in novel lyrical metres such as those imitated by Chiabrera from the French.

[2] See Appendix B for specimens from *Il Pastor Fido* and *L'Adamo*.

rhyme in semi-lyrical dialogues provide parallels to Milton's use of rhyme in his choruses; and, since Milton knew *L'Adamo* at the time when he first seriously meditated on subjects for tragedies, it may well have contributed to his views on methods of imitating the Greek Chorus. When he came to write his tragedy he had long left behind any intention to emulate the *sacre rappresentazioni*, and fixed upon the strict dramatic ideal of Greek tragedy; in his realization of this ideal in *Samson* any lingering notions left by Andreini's dramatic poem were caught up into much more closely controlled and highly organized verse-forms.

IV

Milton did not follow Guarini in making his mono-strophic choruses rhyme throughout; the only example of such a chorus in *Samson Agonistes* is the last, which is only fourteen lines long. Milton's practice moves between the type of semi-lyrical verse used by the Italians in dialogue and the emphatically lyrical tone of their more highly rhymed choruses. He passes from one to the other, aided in this by his adoption of the Greek structure for his play. As in Trissino's *Sofonisba*, the chorus remains on the scene throughout and participates in the dialogue: it so is made to open the new Act after having sung its comments on the last, and this is the function of such lines as:

> But see here comes thy reverend Sire
> With careful step, Locks white as doune,
> Old *Manoah*: advise
> Forthwith how thou oughtst to receive him.
>
> (*S.A.*, ll. 326–9)

and

> But who is this, what thing of Sea or Land?
> Femal of sex it seems
> That so bedeckt, ornate, and gay
> Comes this way sailing
> Like a stately Ship   (S.A., ll. 710–15)

and

> But had we best retire, I see a storm?   (S.A., l. 1060)

Here we are meant to feel the passage from chanted verse to spoken, as in Samson's opening soliloquy from speech to chant in:

> O dark, dark, dark, amid the blaze of noon,
> Irrecoverably dark, total Eclipse
> Without all hope of day!   (S.A., ll. 80–83)

Rhyme is not used in these 'spoken' passages.

If we remind ourselves of the difference in rhyming capacity between Italian and English, we can see that there is the same relationship between, say, Guarini's partly rhymed speeches and his rhymed monostrophic choruses as between these spoken passages by Milton's chorus and its chants. Milton uses no rhyme in the spoken passages, and relatively few in the choruses proper: Guarini's choruses are fully, his speeches partly, rhymed. This is due to the facility of rhyme in Italian, 'which hath scarcely prose', and its relative difficulty in English. The advantage to Milton of this difficulty is that a few rhymes in English have more effect than the same number in Italian: his use of rhyme in these choruses is an enrichment of their music out of all proportion to the number of words which actually rhyme.

For if we read the choruses to discover to what degree they are rhymed, we find that it is generally to a less degree than we would have thought. Thus in Samson's monody, 'O dark, dark, dark, amid the blaze of noon', there is no emphatic use of rhyme at all. The rhyme-words ('noon' with 'Moon', and 'night', 'sight', 'light', 'light') are so placed in the texture of the whole that we cannot feel that they are important. One of the characteristics of rhyme when it appears in the choruses is that it is emphatic, and therefore unmistakable. So the first unmistakable rhyme in the play occurs in the following lines of the chorus which follows Samson's soliloquy:

> *Chalybean* temper'd steel, and frock of mail
> Adamantean Proof;
> But safest he who stood aloof,   (*S.A.*, ll. 133-5)

where its structural purpose, as providing a link and a renewed impetus, is particularly evident.[1] It has been preceded by nineteen unrhymed lines and it is followed by twenty-four more before another emphatic rhyme:

> Shut up from outward light
> To incorporate with gloomy night;   (*S.A.*, ll. 160-1)

and eight lines without rhyme then lead to the conclusion of six lines, in which the rhymes, strong in themselves, are emphasized by the rhythms:

> For him I reckon not in high estate
> Whom long descent of birth
> Or the sphear of fortune raises;
> But thee whose strength, while vertue was her mate
> Might have subdu'd the Earth,
> Universally crown'd with highest praises.
>   (*S.A.*, ll. 170-5)

---

[1] The place and effect of the second rhyme here are those of the *chiave* of a *canzone*; and Milton's use of rhyme in these choruses is affected by the 'rhetoric of rhyme' mentioned in connexion with *Lycidas* (see p. 85).

In the next chorus, 'Just are the ways of God', there is one rhyme, which is emphatic, in the first stanza of seven lines; two rhymes, equally emphatic, in the next stanza, of six lines; none in the next, of eight lines; one which is unemphatic, in the next seven lines; and none in the remaining few lines of the whole.

Rhyme becomes more frequent and obtrusive in the chorus on the deficiencies of women and in the conclud/ing choruses, which celebrate the triumph of Samson's death: in the first of these Milton wishes to gain the effect of sardonic animation, and in the others a note of exalted finality.

The deliberation and skill with which Milton varies the incidence of rhyme to suit the mood and structure of each passage indicate that here we have once more a case of his bettering his instructions; for in none of the Italian exemplars, whether of semi/lyrical speech or of monostrophic choruses, do we find effects so varied and so memorable. Once more Milton, having acquired certain principles, develops them and applies them with absolute confidence.

v

Milton's freedom in the use of rhyme is surpassed by the freedom of his rhythms, which in themselves would give his choruses an advantage over the Italians; but his rhythms, no less than his rhymes, can be inter/preted as a development, but in this case a much bolder development, of Italian form.

Nobody could appreciate Italian verse as Milton did without appreciating that within the traditional limits of the combination of hendecasyllables and hepta/syllables there is scope for far greater rhythmic variety

than within the corresponding English ten-syllable and
six-syllable lines. This greater rhythmic scope goes with
the use of elision in Italian; but the conventions of
elision are in a way fictional, for the resulting lines
should not be read as if to produce uniformity of
rhythm. Rather does the beauty of Italian verse consist
in the real differences of rhythm which result among
lines which are theoretically equivalent. Take the
following two stanzas from Tasso's Chorus in *Aminta*,
O bel età dell' oro:

> Allor tra fiori e linfe
> Traean dolci carole
> Gli Amoretti senz' archi e senza faci:
> Sedean pastori e ninfe,
> Meschiando alle parole
> Vezzi e susurri, ed ai susurri i baci
> Strettamente tenaci:
> La verginella ignude
> Scoprìa sue fresche rose,
> Ch'or tien nel velo ascose,
> E le poma del seno acerbe e crude:
> E spesso in fonte, o in lago
> Scherzar si vide con l'amata il vago.
>
> Tu prima, Onor, velasti
> La fonte dei diletti,
> Negando l'onde all' amorosa sete:
> Tu a' begli occhi insegnasti
> Di starne in se retti,
> E tener lor bellezze altrui secrete:
> Tu raccogliesti in rete
> Le chiome all' aura sparte:
> Tu i dolci atti lascivi
> Festi ritrosi e schivi;
> Ai detti il fren ponesti, ai passi l'arte:
> Opra è tua sola, o Onore,
> Che furto sia quel che fu don d'Amore.[1]

[1] *Opere*, vol. ii, *Aminta*, pp. 37–38.

In the heptasyllabic lines only one (*Strettamente tenaci*) has the theoretic minimum of seven syllables; several have nine or ten syllables and can therefore be read with four stresses, or at least given a rhythm which is plainly freer than usual:

> *Meschiando alle parole*
>
> *Scoprìa sue fresche rose,*
>
> *E spesso in fonte, o in lago*
>
> *Tu a' begli occhi insegnasti*
>
> *Tu i dolci atti lascivi*
>
> *Opra è tua sola, o Onore*

are examples of this mounting of a rhythm of four stresses on a presumed basis of three stresses. The variety of rhythm in the hendecasyllables is scarcely less, but the shorter lines serve better to show how it comes about.

It seems likely that Milton, having done what he could to imitate the freedom of Italian hendecasyllabic rhythms within the limits of the English decasyllable, decided that he could find an equivalent for more lyrical movements only by using a variety of lengths of line. That it was always his instinct to do this in lyrical verse is apparent from such early experiments as *On Time* and *At a Solemn Musick*, where he emulates Italian madrigals and epigrams with the help of octosyllables and alexandrines, as well as lines of ten and six syllables.[1] In *Lycidas* he had indeed used the established English combination of ten-syllable and six-syllable lines to obtain the effect of the traditional Italian combination. But between *Lycidas* and *Samson* there inter-

[1] See p. 64.

vened his strenuous exercise in 'magnificence', in crowd-
ing the utmost variety of movement and sound into the
space of the 'English Heroic Verse'; and one feels that
this immense development of his power of creating
rhythms left him with a reserve of unexplored possibilities, which were suggested to him by the blank
verse of *Paradise Lost*, but which could not be realized
within its limits. The almost wanton variety of rhythms
in the choruses of *Samson* is his expression of these accumulated impulses.

Instead of a theoretic maximum of ten syllables to the
line and a theoretic minimum of six syllables, which is
the normal English version of the traditional Italian
combination, Milton extends both the upper and the
lower limits. He makes his longest line the alexandrine,
and allows himself to descend (though somewhat rarely)
to lines of four or five syllables, such as:

O're worn and soild:	(*S.A.*, l. 123.)
Unclean, unchaste,	(*S.A.*, l. 321.)
To th' inmost mind,	(*S.A.*, l. 610.)
In crude old age;	(*S.A.*, l. 700.)

Between these extremes he allows himself every variety
of length and movement.

The resulting verse can scarcely be called superior or
inferior to the Italian in its possibilities, for its basis has
been changed and the music obtained is essentially
different. The chief difference is that in Milton's
choruses there is none of that rhythmic counterpoint
which comes from the mounting of one particular
rhythm on a presumed norm. This rhythmic tension,
as it may be called, is characteristic of the traditional
Italian prosody; it is replaced in Milton by a freer ebb
and flow, which enables him to bring under one rule
a greater variety of lyric measures. Apart from the

many choruses which develop the movement of Italian hendecasyllables and heptasyllables in combination, there is, for example, a firm tramping rhythm such as this:

> Thy words to my remembrance bring
> How *Succoth* and the Fort of *Penuel*
> Thir great Deliverer contemn'd,
> The matchless *Gideon* in pursuit
> Of *Madian* and her vanquisht Kings:
>
> (S.A., ll. 277-81.)

and the exultant rocking movement of:

> Oh how comely it is and how reviving
> To the Spirits of just men long opprest!
> When God into the hands of thir deliverer
> Puts invincible might
> To quell the mighty of the Earth, th' oppressour,
> The brute and boist'rous force of violent men
> Hardy and industrious to support
> Tyrannic power, but raging to pursue
> The righteous and all such as honour Truth;
>
> (S.A., ll. 1268-76.)

The suggestion of varying musical patterns is heightened by the contrast with the sober movement of the blank-verse dialogue. This is dramatic verse throughout, and the choruses are made dramatic by a disciplined improvisation of the kind which Milton favoured in all his lyric verse after the lines *Upon the Circumcision*.

VI

The metrical analysis of the choruses thus brings out that they have something in common with some of Milton's very early experiments, written perhaps thirty years before. And they also share with the lines *On*

Time and *At a Solemn Musick* a discernible debt to
Spenser. Not that we must imagine Milton consciously
looking back to Spenser's metrical experiments at this
late stage, when he had long achieved a mastery of his
own. But the metrical limitations he sets himself in
Samson reveal the degree to which his whole conception of the music of English verse had been founded
upon Spenser's achievement. For the upper and lower
limits of line which we have described as one of the
bases of the choruses in *Samson* can be seen also in one
of Spenser's lyrics: the stanza he invented for the dirge
in the *November* eclogue of *The Shepheardes Calender*.
Here too there is the upper limit of the alexandrine with
which the stanza begins, and the lower limit of the
two-stressed line with which it ends: the combination
of these line-lengths with lines of five stresses and of
four produces a solemn and varied music:

> *Dido* is gone afore (whose turne shall be the next?)
> There liues shee with the blessed Gods in blisse,
> There drincks she *Nectar* with *Ambrosia* mixt,
> And ioyes enioyes, that mortall men doe misse.
> The honor now of highest gods she is,
>   That whilome was poore shepheards pryde,
>   While here on earth she did abyde.
>   O happy herse,
> Ceasse now my song, my woe now wasted is.
>   O joyfull verse.[1]

The dirge for Dido is one of Spenser's most original
and elaborate experiments; its relation to the *canzone* is
apparent both in the rhyme-scheme (the last six lines
of the stanza are linked to the first four by means of
key-rhymes) and in the varied movement caused by the
different lengths of line. But Spenser, like Milton later,

---

[1] Edmund Spenser, *Poetical Works* (Oxford, 1947), p. 462.

realized that in English verse it was possible and desirable to adopt a greater variety of line-lengths than in
Italian, and in this poem gives special prominence to
the effects thus obtainable.

The opening of Spenser's stanzas here, with their repeated smooth energy, are strongly suggestive of many
such opening alexandrines in Milton's choruses. And
here perhaps one should point out Milton's obvious
fondness for the alexandrine, and for the alexandrine
used as Spenser discovered it could be used: as an
intermittent but regular and powerful reinforcement of
the usual line-lengths. For some reason Milton ex-
cluded it from *Lycidas*. There was no place for it in his
blank verse or in the sonnets. But he takes it up with
enthusiasm in *Samson* and uses it with many of its
different cadences, but most often with the rolling
resonance which Spenser too had found to be one of
its capacities. When Spenser wrote

> The warres he well remembred of king *Nine*,
> Of old *Assarachus*, and *Inachus* divine,

he prepared the way for some of the most resounding
of Milton's lines in these choruses.

VII

Yet there is one final observation to be made on the
apparent freedom of the choruses in *Samson*, and that
will lead to a deeper analysis of their structure. It is
that, in spite of their almost wanton variety of rhythm
and pattern, their freedom is of a solidified massive kind
which corresponds to the freedom of Milton's blank
verse: it is a legal, or even legalistic, freedom, which

comes at times to seem no freedom at all, but a most ironic form of captivity. Everyone feels that the choruses in *Samson* disport themselves according to law, though few have been able to detect, or at least to formulate, the code which governs them. Their self-licensed liberty of movement is not, of course, to be distinguished entirely from the self-imposed artifice of their language. Any liberty which Milton sought would naturally be restricted by his notions of 'magnificence', of decorum, of using 'English words in a foreign idiom'. But the strangely limited liberty of these choruses may be related directly to their metrical basis, to their being, as the blank verse of *Paradise Lost* is, based upon Italian prosody.

That prosody is based upon rhyme, even when rhyme disappears, as in *versi sciolti*, or is used but sparingly, as in the semi-lyrical passages of the dramas. It has been suggested that traces of the influence of rhyme are to be found in the line-endings in Milton's blank verse, where we find that the tenth syllable is the pivot of the line and must be given a word such as would be either a good sonorous rhyme-word or capable of being given a certain stress.[1] The same influence is seen at work in the choruses of *Samson Agonistes*, and demonstrates their kinship, not only to Milton's blank verse in general, but to the Italian originals of both.

The Italians may be said to have made the discovery that in a prosody based on rhyme one might write lyric verse which was lightly or only occasionally rhymed, provided that one retained or heightened the diction and movement of lyric poetry. Milton has but applied this discovery to English, dropping the Italian conventions of elision and allowing himself, as a substitute

[1] See p. 135.

for these, a greater variety of line-lengths in his choral verse.

But one essential feature of the Italian prosody must be kept: that is, the provision, in the last place of the line, of a word which is as weighty as a rhyme-word.[1] This word provided, it is a matter of indifference whether the line rhymes or not: indeed, perhaps the effect is better if it usually does *not* rhyme, for then a kind of surprise results, an effect of continuous expectation which impels the verses forward. At the same time these rich or heavy terminations are satisfying in themselves. Consider the third stanza of the chorus 'Just are the ways of God':

> As if they would confine th' interminable,
> And tie him to his own prescript,
> Who made our Laws to bind us, not himself,
> And hath full right to exempt
> Whom so it pleases him by choice
> From National obstriction, without taint
> Of sin, or legal debt;
> For with his own Laws he can best dispence.
>
> (S.A., ll. 307–14.)

The line-endings are full of double consonants, most of them dentals and labials, and the effect of rhyme is so strongly suggested (especially since the first two stanzas have both included emphatic rhymes) that one has to look twice to discover that what we have here is not rhyme, but assonance, and that perhaps not wholly intentional.

[1] Endings such as these:
    'Spurn'd them to death by Troops. The bold *Ascalonite*'
or
    'A thousand fore-skins fell, the flower of *Palestin*'
are not exceptions, whether they occur in alexandrines or not; for they may either be treated as *sdruccioli*, as in the blank verse line:
    'Such solitude above sweetest society'
or it may be said that their last syllable could perfectly well be made to rhyme if necessary.

One might say, then, that the secret of the music of this verse is that it is rhymed verse which does not rhyme, or unrhymed verse which seems to do so: whichever description we prefer, the intermittent occurrence of full rhyme is essential to the total effect. Without it we should feel a haunting uneasiness or sense of frustration, as of an expectation too consistently cheated. With it, we are confirmed in our attention, and our expectation is rewarded at intervals by the sometimes emphatic completion of the rhyme:

> Nor only dost degrade them, or remit
> To life obscur'd, which were a fair dismission,
> But throw'st them lower then thou didst exalt them high,
> Unseemly falls in human eie,
> Too grievous for the trespass or omission,
>
> (*SA*., ll. 687–9.)

This discovery that a lineending can be obtrusive either by the absence or the presence of rhyme[1] corresponds to Milton's earlier discovery, first applied in the sonnets and elaborated in his blank verse, that a lineending can be emphatic both when the sentence ends with it and when it does not: indeed, that the more accustomed the sentence is to disregard the limits of the line, the more those limits impose themselves, in a kind of counterpoint, on the consciousness of the reader.

This peculiar exploitation of rhyme could perhaps have been discovered only in Italian, where it is diffi

---

[1] Examples in which the absence of rhyme is a particularly striking effect are not hard to find: I find one in the last line of this passage:

> So fond are mortal men
> Fall'n into wrath divine,
> As thir own ruin on themselves to invite,
> Insensate left, or to sense reprobate,
> And with blindness internal struck.
>
> (*S.A.*, ll. 1682–6).

cult to find a word which does not rhyme with an enormous number of others. In the *Aminta* or the *Pastor Fido* the music of the partly rhymed speeches derives from the fact that the line-endings are unmistakably and inevitably all rhyme-words. Yet oddly enough, this discovery was not exploited in Italian for some considerable time, perhaps because Italian poetry very soon entered on a phase of prolonged enervation. It is not until the later *Canti* of Leopardi that we find the development of a lyric form based upon the same principles as Milton's choruses in *Samson*; and the origins of these may even be shared by Leopardi's odes, for Leopardi invented the form after experimenting with brief imitations of the choruses in *Aminta* and the *Pastor Fido*.[1]

[1] *I Canti di Giacomo Leopardi*, commentati da Alfredo Straccali, third edition (Firenze, 1911). See the commentary on the two fragments translated from Simonides, Nos. XXI and XXII in this edition.

APPENDIX A

Specimens of Sixteenth-century Italian Epic Blank Verse

A. From Trissino's *L'Italia liberata dai Goti*, begun *c.* 1527, published 1547–8

L'altissimo Signor, che 'l ciel governa,
Si stava un dì fra le Beate genti,
Risguardando i negozi de' mortali,
Quando un' alma virtù, che Providenza
Da voi si chiama, sospirando, disse:
  O caro Padre mio, da cui dipende
Ogni opra, che si fa là giuso in terra,
Non vi muove pietà, quando mirate,
Che la misera Italia già tant' anni
Vive suggetta ne le man de' Gotti?
Egli è pur mal, che la più bella parte
Del mondo se ritruovi in tanti affanni,
In tanta servitù senza soccorso.
Pur è passato il destinato tempo,
Che permesso fu a gli Angeli nocivi,
Ch'inducessero in lei tanta ruina,
Per penitenza dei commessi errori.
Or che la pena avanza ogni delitto,
Fatela, Signor mio, libera, e sciolta,
Come talor mi fu per voi promesso.
  Rispose, sorridendo, il Padre eterno:
Figliuola, il tuo pensier molto m'aggrada;
Non dubitar, che già vicino è 'l tempo,
Da doversi eseguir la mia promessa;
Che ciò ch'io dico, e con la testa affermo,
Non può mancar per accidente alcuno.[1]

[1] From Book I: reproduced in Giangiorgio Trissino, *Scritti Scelti* (Vicenza, 1950), pp. 90–91.

Translation. The most high Lord who rules the Heavens was standing one day among the blessed nations, looking upon the affairs of mortal men, when a gentle virtue which is called Providence by you, sighing said:

'O dear Father of mine, on whom depends every action that is done there below on earth, are you not moved by pity when you see that unhappy Italy now for so many years lives subjected to the hands of the Goths? 'Tis indeed ill, that the loveliest region of the world should find itself in such woes, without redress in such a servitude. And yet the destined time is passed, which was allowed to the evil Angels, who brought such ruin upon her, in punishment for the errors she had committed. Now that the penalty surpasses any crime, my Lord, let her be set free and unbound, as it was one time promised me by you.'

Answered, smiling, the eternal Father: 'Daughter, thy thought much pleases me. Doubt not that now near is the time when my promise must be carried out; for what I say and affirm with a nod, can never fail by any accident.'

Comment. Benedetto Croce has called Trissino's poem an involuntary parody of the *Iliad*. In the above extract both thought and presentation are pedestrian. The diction is plain and sometimes flat. The word-order is as near to that of simple speech as is possible in verse. The sentences more often than not pause at the line-endings, and there is no attempt to produce any special sonority or tension in the metre.

B. From Annibal Caro's *Eneide*, completed in 1565-6, published in 1581

> Nel primo entrar del doloroso regno
> Stanno il Pianto, l'Angoscia, e le voraci
> Cure; e i pallidi Morbi e 'l duro Affanno
> Con la debil Vecchiezza. Evvi la Tema,
> Evvi la Fame; una ch'è freno al bene,
> L'altra stimolo al male; orrendi tutti
> E spaventosi aspetti. Avvi il Disagio,

La Povertà, la Morte, e de la Morte
Parente, il Sonno. Avvi de' cor non sani
Le non sincere Gioie. Avvi la Guerra,
De le genti omicida, e de le Furie
I ferrati còvili, il Furor folle,
L'empia Discordia, che di serpi ha 'l crine,
E di sangue mai sempre il volto intriso.

   Nel mezzo erge le braccia annose al cielo
Un olmo opaco e grande, ove si dice
Che s'annidano i Sogni, e ch'ogni fronda
V'ha la sua vana imago e 'l suo fantasma.
Molte, oltre a ciò, vi son di varie fere
Mostruose apparenze. In su le porte
I biformi centauri, e le biformi
Due Scille, Briarèo di cento doppi;
La Chimera di tre, che con tre bocche
Il foco avventa; il gran serpe di Lerna
Con sette teste; e con tre corpi umani
Erilo e Geriòne; e con Medusa
Le Gòrgoni sorelle; e l'empie Arpìe,
Che son vergini insieme, augelli e cagne.[1]

Translation. At the first entrance to the dolorous realm stand
Weeping, Anguish, and voracious Care, and the pale Diseases
and hard Toil with weak Old Age. There is Fear, there Hun-
ger, the one a curb to Good, the other a spur to Evil; all fearful
and horrible in their aspects. There too is Unease, Poverty,
Death and, parent of Death, Sleep. There are the not sincere
Joys of hearts not whole. There are War, slayer of nations, and
the iron-bound dens of the Furies, foolish Rage, impious Discord, who has snakes for locks and face never unstained by
blood.

In the midst lifts up its twisted arms to Heaven a vast and
shadowy oaktree, where 'tis said Dreams nest, and every leaf
has there its vain image and its phantasm. Many, further than
this, are the monstrous apparitions there. Above the gates
biform Centaurs and the twin biform Scillas; Briareus with the

[1] *L'Eneide, tradotta da Annibal Caro* (Firenze, 1914), p. 113.

hundred folds; the Chimera with three, which from three mouths breathes fire; the great serpent of Lerna with seven heads; and with three human bodies Erilo and Geryon; and with Medusa, the sisters the Gorgons; and the impious Harpies, who are at once virgins, birds and dogs.

Comment. Caro has latinized his vocabulary and his idiom. He has attempted to imitate the movement of Virgil's hexa-meters by introducing strong pauses at different points within his lines. There is a certain ruggedness and irregularity of rhythm, obtained largely by the collocation of open vowels. He seeks also to imitate the inversions, suspensions, and repetitions of Virgil's diction.

C. From Tasso's *Le Sette Giornate del Mondo Creato*, completed
1594

> Poi benedisse Dio la cara imago
> Di se, da se creata, e disse appresso:
> Crescete in numerosa, e bella prole:
> Riempite la terra, e lei soggetta
> Fate all' arbitrio vostro, al vostro impero:
> Signoreggiate in mar gli umidi pesci,
> E ne i campi dell' aria i vaghi augelli:
> E qualunque animal si move in terra
> Soggetto fia non meno al vostro regno.
> In questa guisa tu creato appena,
> Uom, creato Re fosti; e l'alto impero,
> E la sublime potestate impressa
> Non ti fu data in secco, o fragil legno,
> O nelle pieghe pur di breve carta,
> Perchè la roda al fin putrido verme;
> Ma la Natura scritta in se riserba
> L'alta voce divina, e 'l chiaro suono.
> Comandi, e 'l naturale, e giusto impero
> In terra estenda, e dentro al mar sonante,
> E nel sublime ancor dell' aria vaga.
> Imperioso tu nascesti in prima.

Or perchè dunque servi a' propri affetti,
E la tua dignità disprezzi, e perdi,
Ligio omai fatto del peccato, e servo?
Perchè te stesso prigionier cattivo
Fai di Satan, in sue catene avvolto;
Se già nascendo sei Principe detto
Delle cose create, e Re terrestre?
Perchè, quasi gettando, a terra spargi
Quel, ch'a nostra natura in se più degno
Di riverenza, e di sublime onore?
Qual' all' imperio tuo prescritto in terra
È fine, o pur nell' aria, o 'n mar profondo?
Se ben te stesso, e lui misuri, e scorgi,
Non hai tu penne da volar nel Cielo;
Ma l'ardita ragion nulla ritiene.
Questa con l'ali sue trapassa a volo,
Non pur dell' aria i più ventosi campi,
Ma del Cielo gli stellanti, ed aurei chiostri.
E via men cupo, e men profondo 'l mare
È del suo peregrino, e vago ingegno,
Che va spiando dentro a' salsi regni
I secreti dell' onde, e i seni, e i fondi,
E le sue occulte meraviglie: e quindi
Vittorioso alfin ritorna in alto,
Di saper ricco, e d'immortal tesoro.
Così per arte dell' umano ingegno
Prende tutte le cose, e fa soggette.[1]

Translation. Then God blessed the dear image of Himself, by Him created, and said forthwith: 'Increase in numerous and lovely off-spring: fill full the Earth and make it subject to your judgement, to your rule: reign over the moist fish in the sea and the fair birds in the fields of the air: and whatever animal moves on the earth shall be subjected no less to your reign.' Thus thou scarcely created, Man, wast created King; and the high empire, and sublime power impressed on thee, was not given to thee on a dry and fragile piece of wood, or even in the

[1] *Le Sette Giornate del Mondo Creato* (Londra, 1780), pp. 284–5.

folds of a brief paper, so that it might be gnawed at last by a putrid worm; but Nature written in herself reserves the high voice of God, and the clear sound. Rule, and thy natural and just empire extend on earth and within the sounding sea, and even in the sublime heights of the shining air. Thou wast born at first imperious. Now wherefore then art slave to thy own desires, and dost despise thy dignity and losest it, henceforth made liegeman and slave to sin? Why dost thou make thyself an evil prisoner to Satan, involved in his chains, if even at birth thou wast said to be a Prince, and terrestrial King? Why, as it were casting it on earth, scatterest thou what our nature has in it most worthy of reverence and sublime honour? What limit is written to thy rule on earth, or even in the air, or the deep sea? If well thou measur'st and discern'st thyself and the Heavens, thou hast no wings to fly in the sky; but daring reason is held back by nothing. She with her wings traverses in flight, not only the windiest fields of the air, but the starry and golden cloisters of the sky. And far less hollow and less profound is the sea than her wandering and eager spirit, which goes seeking out in the briny regions the secrets of the waves, and the ocean's bosom and the deeps, and their hidden marvels: and thence victorious at last returns on high, rich in wisdom and immortal treasures. So [Man] by the skill of human intellect takes all things and makes them subject to himself.

Comment. The length of the verse-paragraph illustrates rather Tasso's volubility than his capacity to build up a unified series of lines. Yet even this expansiveness shows that he has devised a formula, a type of diction and rhetoric which can be used to elevate and inflate his matter.[1] This passage may serve to exemplify the more pedestrian sections of his poem. Despite the conscious nobility of the thought, the verse does not rise to a convincing exaltation. It may be noticed in this passage how great a disadvantage it is to him not to have a narrative to clothe in this 'magnificent' blank verse. The ponderous qualities of the style are most obvious in argument and reflection, especially when these are neither ingenious nor powerful.

[1] For a description of Tasso's diction and prosody see pp. 51-4.

D. From *Il Diluvio*, by Gabriello Chiabrera, published in
1598

E già di nubi tenebroso oscuro
Velo si stende, e se ne copre il volto
Chiaro del giorno, e da l'aeree fonti
Spandesi immensa, insuperabil pioggia;
Tanta non mai, benchè Orion superbo
L'aria turbasse, e procelloso Arturo
Ne l'alto risorgesse onda si sparse;
Immantenente i seminati campi
Furo dispersi, e la fidata messe
Per gli aratori al grembo de la terra
Tutta predaro i turbini celesti;
L'alte foreste de gran gioghi alpini
Svelte cadean, che già cento anni, e cento
Guerreggiaro con l'impero de' venti;
Usciva homai di sua sembianza il mondo;
Onda era il piano, onda la valle, ed onda
Già quasi i monti, e dentro l'onde errando
Sparse perdeansi le superbie humane.
Gli uomini di pallor tinti le guancie,
E freddi il sangue infra le vene, il piede
Moveano intorno a procurar salute;
Chi sosteneva il genitore antico,
Chi porgea mano a le consorti, ed elle
Versando in sul bel petto amari pianti
Stringeansi al seno i pargoletti infermi;
Così movean le sbigottite turbe
Inverso i monti, e colà suso in cima
Altri piangea dolente i suoi tesori,
Altri gli amor di alma bellezza, ed altri
La sommersa carissima famiglia;
Era chi vago rimirava l'acque
Tanto diffuse, e si scriveva in mente
L'acerba vista de l'orribil caso,
Per farne historia a successor nipoti;
Lasso, ma van fu suo sperar, ch'al fine

Salendo l'onda imperiosa ascose
Tutto egualmente il volto de la terra;
Solo infra le procelle, infra gli abissi,
Infra i tuoni, infra i turbini, infra i lampi,
Allor tutta secura, e reverita
Notava l'arca; ed ascoltando i gridi
De cor sommersi, e l'orrido rimbombo
De l'onde irate, il buon Noè tranquillo
Canta la forza del Signor superno . . .[1]

Translation. And now a shadowy obscure veil of clouds
stretches out, and the clear face of day is covered over, and from
the aerial founts pours forth an immense, insuperable rain;
great as never before, though proud Orion disturbed the air,
and tempestuous Arcturus risen in the deep scattered waves(?);
forthwith the sown fields were dispersed and the harvest en-
trusted by the ploughmen to the earth's bosom was all seized
by the heavenly whirlwinds; the high forests fell torn from the
great alpine slopes, which for hundreds and hundreds of years
had warred with the power of the winds; the world now
abandoned its wonted appearance; the plain was water, water the
valley, and water already almost the mountains, and within the
waves, wandering, the pride of men was scattered and lost. Men
with their cheeks tinged with pallor, their blood cold within
their veins, hastened their steps to seek safety; some sustained their
aged parent, some lent a hand to their wives, and these shedding
bitter tears in their fair bosoms clasped to their breasts their
feeble children; thus moved the terrified multitudes towards the
mountains, and there above on the summits some wept grieving
over their treasures. Some wept for their lovers of sweetest beauty,
and some for their dear drowned family. There were some who
eagerly gazed on the far-spread waters, and noted in their minds
the fearful sight of the horrible disaster, in order to tell it as a story
to their descendants; alas, but vain was their hope, for at last the
imperious wave rising hid equally the whole face of the earth;
alone among the tempests, among the abysses, among the thun-
ders, among the whirlwinds, among the lightnings, then all

[1] *Poemetti di Gabriello Chiabrera* (Firenze, 1598), pp. 32–33.

secure and respected swam the Ark; and hearkening the cries of those who drowned, and the horrid roaring of the angry waves, good Noah in peace sang the power of the eternal Lord . . .

Comment. Chiabrera's verse is not distinguished by any personal touches from that of Caro and Tasso; it is rather evidence of the general acceptance, by the end of the century, of this type of blank verse as a formula. These five short narrative poems seem to be exercises in the heroic verse-tradition established by Tasso to express the militant religious fervour of the Counter-Reformation. Each is an heroic or pious episode: David's challenge to Goliath, the liberation of St. Peter, David slaying the lion, the Deluge, and the conversion of Mary Magdalene. Chiabrera's chief epic resource is the Homeric simile. His true genius found expression in lyrical verse, and the *sciolti* of these poems are mechanical, if efficient. There is, however, a generic resemblance between this blank verse and Milton's, both in style and execution and in intellectual and religious content: it may serve to indicate Milton's remarkable kinship with the Italians of the Counter-Reformation.

APPENDIX B

Specimens of the Verse of *Il Pastor Fido*
and *L'Adamo*

A. Concluding Chorus of Act III of Guarini's *Il Pastor Fido*

Come sei grande, Amore,
Di natura miracolo, e del mondo!
Qual cor sì rozzo, o qual sì fiera gente
Il tuo valor non sente?
Ma qual sì scaltro ingegno, e sì profondo
Il tuo valor intende?
Chi sa gli ardori, che 'l tuo foco accende
Importuni, e lascivi,
Dirà, Spirto mortal, tu regni, e vivi
Ne la corporea salma;
Ma chi sa poi come a virtù l'amante
Si desti, e come soglia
Farsi al tuo foco (ogni sfrenata voglia
Subito spenta) pallido e tremante;
Dirà, Spirto immortale, hai tu ne l'alma
Il tuo solo, e santissimo ricetto?
Raro mostro, e mirabile, d'umano,
E di divino aspetto,
Di veder cieco, e di saver insano,
Di senso, e d'intelletto,
Di ragione, e desio confuso affetto!

E tale hai tu l'impero
De la terra, e del ciel, ch'a te soggiace.
Ma (dirol con tua pace)
Miracolo più altero
Ha di te il mondo, e più stupendo assai;
Però che quanto fai
Di maraviglia, e di stupor tra noi
Tutto in virtù di bella donna puoi.

O donna, o don del cielo,
Anzi pur di colui,
Che 'l tuo leggiadro velo
Fè, d'ambo creator, più bel di lui:
Qual cosa non hai tu del ciel più bella?
Ne la sua vasta fronte,
Mostruoso Ciclope, un occhio ei gira,
Non di luce a chi 'l mira,
Ma d'alta cecità cagione, e fonte;
Se sospira, o favella
Com' irato leon rugge, e spaventa,
E non più ciel, ma campo
Di tempestosa, ed horrida procella
Col fiero lampeggiar folgori avventa.
Tu col soave lampo,
E con la vista angelica amorosa
Di due soli visibili, e sereni,
L'anima tempestosa
Di chi ti mira acqueti, e rassereni:
E suono, e moto, e lume,
E valor, e bellezza, e leggiadria,
Fan sì dolce armonia nel tuo bel viso,
Che 'l cielo in van presume,
Se 'l cielo è pur men bel del Paradiso,
Di pareggiarsi a te, cosa divina.
E ben ha gran ragione
Quel altero animale,
Ch'uomo s'appella, ed a cui pur s'inchina
Ogni cosa mortale,
Se mirando di te l'alta cagione
S'inchina, e cede, e s'ei trionfa, e regna,
Non è perchè di scettro, o di vittoria
Sii tu di lui men degna,
Ma per maggior tua gloria.
Che quanto il vinto è di più pregio, tanto
Più glorioso è di chi vince il vanto.

Ma che la tua beltate
Vinca con l'uomo ancor l'umanitate,

Oggi ne fà Mirtillo a chi nol crede
Meravigliosa fede,
E mancava ben questo al tuo valore,
Donna di far senza speranza amore.

Translation. How art thou, O Love, the miracle of Nature, and the world! What heart is so harsh, or what nation so fierce, that they feel not thy worth? But what mind is so swift and so profound that it can understand thy worth? He who knows the importunate and longing ardours which thy fire kindles, will say, O mortal spirit, thou livest and reignest in the bodily form; but he who knows then how the lover wakes to virtue and how he will become pale and trembling at thy fire, all unbridled desire suddenly extinguished, will say, ·O immortal spirit, hast thou in the soul thy only and most holy dwelling-place? Rare and wondrous monster, of both divine and human aspect, seeing in blindness and being wise in madness, confused emotion of sense, of intellect, of reason and desire!

And as such thou hast the rule over earth, and heaven, which lie subject to thee. But (I say it with respect) a prouder wonder than thee the world yet holds, and a more stupendous; for all thou dost of wonder and mystery among us, thou dost it all by the power of lovely woman.

O woman, O gift of Heaven, or rather of Him who, Creator of both, made thy lovely veil fairer than Man's: what thing hast thou that is not fairer than Heaven? Heaven in its vast brow, like a monstrous Cyclops, rolls one eye, which is a source and occasion of thick blindness, not of light, to him who looks on it; if Heaven sighs or speaks, it roars and terrifies like an angry lion, and (no longer sky, but a field of fearful and horrible tempest) kindles lightnings with its fierce flashing. Thou with thy gentle light, and with the amorous and angelic sight of two visible and serene suns, quietest and soothest the stormy soul of him who gazes on thee: and sound and movement and light and worth and beauty and gaiety make so sweet a harmony in thy fair face, that the sky in vain presumes (if the sky is indeed less than Paradise) to compare itself to thee, thou divine thing. And indeed that proud animal called man, to whom all mortal things bow down, is right if, looking on the high cause thou givest, he bows himself down and yields; and if he triumphs and reigns, it is not because thou art less worthy than he of sceptre and victory, but for thy greater glory; for the greater is the prize that is conquered, the greater is the boast of him who conquers.

But that thy beauty can conquer even Man's humanity, today will be given marvellous proof by Mirtillo to him who believes it not; and this indeed was wanting to thy power, woman, to make love exist without hope.

Comment. This chorus is printed without divisions into para-graphs in the old editions. The organization of the rhymes indicates that, like Milton's choruses, it is meant to fall into irregular sections.

B. The opening of Andreini's *Adamo*

PADRE ETERNO, CORO DE ANGELI

PADRE ETERNO. Alzi dal tetro orror l'orrida fronte
Lucifero dolente a tanta luce;
Abbagli al lampo di fulgenti stelle,
E di non caldo sole aneli a i raggi:
Ne' volumi del ciel legga le tante
Gran meraviglie di celeste mano;   a
Miri il Rubello insano   a
Com' è facile il modo
Al gran fabro de mondi,
De l'alto Empireo sublimar le soglie
Inalzando l'umile
Là 've cadde il superbo: b
Quindi con duolo acerbo   b
(Salamandra infernal, talpi d'orrori)
L'ostinato rimiri,
Disperato suo scampo e mia pietate,
Ne la salute altrui la sua ruina,
E nel chiudersi il ciel, chi s'apre il cielo;
E dal cupo del cor alto sospiro
Traendo al fin (gloria a me dando) dica:

> Ahi ch'al Fattore eccelso
> Misero ben m'avveggio
> Uopo altro non gli fa, che di se stesso
> Per dar ordine al tutto.

SERAFINI *cantanti.*	O superbo apparato, ⟶ a
	E di luna, e di sol gran lumi ornato, ⟶ a
	Ne gli Angeli canoro, ⟶ b
	Ne le sfere sonoro: ⟶ b
	O come vai destando ⟶ c
	A grand' atto d'amore ⟶ d
	L'Uom farsi spettatore. ⟶ d
CHERUBINI *cantanti.*	Nel gran foglio del cielo ⟶ e
	Divo scritto sovrano ⟶ f
	Penna fe' il dito de l'eterna mano, ⟶ f
	E l'opre sue più belle ⟶ g
	Narrando scrisse, e lettre fur le stelle; ⟶ g
	Or queste l'Uom mirando ⟶ h
	Vad' alto sì poggiando, ⟶ h
	Che miri ornato del corporeo velo, ⟶ e
	Che s'ha il piede nel mondo, ha 'l capo in cielo.[1] ⟶ e

Translation.

GOD THE FATHER, CHORUS OF ANGELS

GOD THE FATHER. Let Lucifer, grieving at so much light, lift his horrible brow from black horror; let him be blinded in the light of glowing stars, and pant in the rays of the not fierce sun; let him read in the volumes of the sky the many grand wonders of the heavenly hand; let the mad Rebel see how easy it is for the great Creator of worlds to raise the thresholds of the high Empyrean, lifting up the humble, there where the proud fell: thence with bitter pain (infernal salamander, mole of horrors), let the obstinate one see again, despairing of his escape and of my pity, in others' salvation his own ruin, and how in closing itself [to him], the sky opens [to others]: and from the

---

[1] Filippo Scolari, *Saggio di Critica sul Paradiso Perduto* (Venezia, 1818), pp. 239–40.

depths of his heart drawing at last a deep sigh (giving me glory) let him say: Ah now indeed, me miserable, I see how the most high Creator has need of none but Himself to set all in order.

SERAPHIM *singing*. O splendid frame, adorned with sun and moon, great lights, singing in the Angels, sounding in the spheres: O how thou wakest Man who becomes thy spectator to great acts of love.

CHERUBIM *singing*. On the great page of the sky the divine sovereign Author made a pen of the finger of his eternal hand, and telling of his loveliest works wrote, and the stars were the letters: now let Man, gazing on these, ascend so high in flight that he may see, though wrapped in the body's veil, that, if he has his feet on earth, he has his head in the sky.

Comment. In the dialogue the occasional rhymes are used to articulate the speech, providing links at turning-points.

PRINTED IN GREAT BRITAIN
AT THE UNIVERSITY PRESS, OXFORD
BY VIVIAN RIDLER
PRINTER TO THE UNIVERSITY